AS I SEE IT

THOUGHTS FOR WOMEN ON ISSUES
THAT MATTER FROM
A BIBLICAL PERSPECTIVE

CATHE LAURIE

KERYGMA
PUBLISHING

ALLEN
DAVID
BOOKS

AS I SEE IT

ISBN: 978-1-61291-427-5

Published by: Kerygma Publishing
Coordination: FM Management, Ltd.
Contact: mgf@fmmgt.net
Cover design: Ross Geerdes Design
Photographs of author: Trever Hoehne
Production: Mark Ferjulian

Printed in the United States of America

1 2 3 4 5 6 7 / 18 17 16 15 14 13

FOR GREG

This year marks the thirty-ninth year I have been your friend, wife, lover, colaborer in ministry, walking partner, et cetera, et cetera!

Thirty-nine!

Who knew the funny, joyful, exciting, and, at times, terrifying ride that life would take us on when I said I'd marry you. But then our idea of an exotic honeymoon (to which we both agreed) was Disneyland's Enchanted Tiki Room and a ride on the Matterhorn.

I don't recall that you ever formally proposed. I just remember two pivotal conversations. One was driving home from Idyllwild Camp in your broken-down Corvair. I must have been fifteen, and you eighteen. You said something like, "Well . . . I guess we are boyfriend-girlfriend now. But there's one thing I want you to know: If you *ever* get between me and my relationship with the Lord, it will be over, okay?"

Ha! You were ever the romantic. Believe it or not, I was so happy to hear you say that. I was sick of guys who were wishy-washy.

Then of course there was your official marriage proposal. After breaking up and getting back together three times, it went something like this: "So, I guess we ought to makes plans to tell your mom and dad we want to get married, right?"

Oh sure, they were thrilled. They always wanted me to marry a guy without a steady paycheck who looked like Redbeard the pirate.

Anyway, you knew I wasn't the type to be impressed by a plane's skywriting, "Will you marry me?" or with some crazy treasure hunt to find a buried ring in a box. (What in the world are kids today thinking? Leave some excitement for the marriage already!)

What makes our marriage so fun is that we really are pretty opposite. You are the yin to my yang, the only child to my middle child, the *Hawaii Five-O* to my *Antiques Road Show,* and the Tigger to my Eeyore. You're "the glass is half full" to my "the glass is half empty."

Like I said to you yesterday, I wish I had 10 percent of your optimism!

I love you for a hundred reasons and more.

I have never wondered if you love me.

You make me laugh (and when you couldn't, you still kept trying). You're generous. . . . I've often thought when balancing the checkbook that you are too generous!

I have *never* doubted that you were faithful. I always knew you would put God first before the kids and me. You are kind and forgiving, even when you've been hurt. You are never petty or vindictive.

Okay, okay, enough praise for one day. I think you get the gist of it. . . . I love you with all my heart—more today than ever.

You said it best in a card you gave me forty years ago (remember the dark ages when we used to write things on paper?): "Nothing is better for me than thee."

CONTENTS

FOREWORD

I t's finally here! Cathe Laurie's book.

I can't tell you how many times we have talked about capturing her outstanding thoughts and insights from Scripture and life on paper. Cathe's response has always been something along the lines of, "No one would want to read a book written by me!"

But I remind her that thousands of women listen to her every week as she teaches at Virtue, her Bible study for women. Not only that, but when she writes a blog or does an entry on her Facebook page, so many people respond. That's because Cathe has a gift—a gift to communicate God's truth in an understandable way.

Before you in this book are many of her musings. Some are based on Bible studies she has done, others are blog entries, and many were written specifically for this book. You need to know that Cathe is first and foremost a wife, mother, and grandmother. She delights in being a homemaker. But she also has a calling from God to help others.

The name of her women's ministry, Virtue, is drawn from the description of the woman of virtue in Proverbs 31. The word *virtue,* however, isn't just a feminine term. It is also a word used of men and connotes courage, influence, even force.

Cathe Laurie is a woman of influence.

She is my wife of thirty-nine years and my most trusted

counselor. And now . . . she can offer some of that counsel to you as well.

May God bless this book, using it to touch many lives for His greater glory.

Greg Laurie

PREFACE: SEE LIFE THE WAY IT IS

Not long ago we had a family photo taken at the beach. When we got the print, everyone looked absolutely fantastic . . . except for me! Looking at that photo, I could see every line, every wrinkle, every blemish. I know I must have looked in the mirror that morning, but I obviously hadn't done enough to cover all of the faults and flaws. In fact, I was seeing myself as I really was, and I didn't much like it.

I think it's important that we see things as they are.

That may not be as easy as you would imagine. The truth is, it's often difficult for us to open our eyes to see ourselves and our walk with Christ as they truly are. We all have a tendency to fool ourselves, outright lie to ourselves, or avert our gaze from things we really don't want to see.

The way we can see clearly is to evaluate our lives through the strong lens of the Word of God, examining ourselves by His standards rather than the standards of others . . . or how we would like to see ourselves. Let's face it, we are sometimes quick to gloss over those incidents in our lives when we lose our temper or overindulge or waste our time or make a cutting remark to someone. We will say, "Lord, please forgive me" and then move on with our day. But we haven't really dealt with the sin, and that's why we struggle with it again and again. Let's take off those rose-colored glasses we like to wear and see ourselves as we really are.

That's what I have sought to do in this, my very first book,

As I See It. It's a collection of things I have written about over the years, and quite a few I wrote just for this book.

I have to say that my husband, Greg, would not let me out of writing this.

I didn't feel I really had that much to say, especially in written form, and I certainly didn't feel qualified to write an entire book. But Greg wouldn't hear of it.

He told me that if I had preached it, I could and should write on it as well.

So after some prodding by Greg and, I must admit, some nudging by the Holy Spirit, here it is, *As I See It.*

I hope you will see God in its pages . . . and see yourself better as a result.

Cathe Laurie

1: CHOCOLATE EGGS, PASTEL DRESSES, AND CELEBRATING EASTER

So the women hurried away from the tomb, afraid
yet filled with joy, and ran to tell his disciples.
Suddenly Jesus met them. "Greetings," he said.
They came to him, clasped his feet and worshiped
him.

(MATTHEW 28:8-9, NIV)

I can remember Easter Sundays, growing up in the sixties.

It began with waking up early for Sunday morning and then looking forward to a big Easter brunch and an egg hunt later that day — not to mention all the fuss my parents endured as they tried to get all five of us children spit-spot and ready for church.

I have a snapshot of one such day, showing us kids squinting into the camera as my father took our picture. My two sisters and I were dressed in matching pastel ensembles: mandatory white hats, white gloves, and white lace-trimmed stockings. Fancy Nancy would have loved every minute of it. Me? Not so much.

Those dresses weren't the most comfortable get-ups. They were nipped in tightly at the waistline (too tight, as I never had much of a curvy shape) and were made of fussy fabrics like organza or starched lace. Underneath, voluminous skirts were layers of stiff petticoats that pricked the backs of my thighs when I sat down.

Church in those days was formal and seemed to last an

eternity. To me, it was just plain boring and something to be endured. Sadly, most of what was said that day was lost on a six-year-old girl who spent the time gazing out the window at the beautiful spring day.

Looking back fifty years at the long church service, the discomfort of a tight waistline and being poked by a petticoat are all I remember. But now it takes on new significance. I recognize what it was to have a child's perspective.

My memory of that day stands as a pinpoint along the sweeping timeline of Christian history. Generation after generation has marked that first Sunday morning when Mary Magdalene discovered the stone had been taken away and the tomb was empty. It is the event that defines our faith.

Remembering that Easter from long ago jogged me into praise today. It reminded me that as I sat and fidgeted, distracted and fixated on chocolate eggs, the Lord of glory patiently waited for the significance of Easter to finally dawn on me a decade later.

I have been choosing my own Easter dresses for quite some time now, thank you very much. (This year, it's vibrant orange and made of comfortable fabric in a shape that suits me. Forget the petticoat, gloves, and lace stockings.)

Like the child of long ago, I still grumble and complain. I still get distracted and fidget, fixating on things that aren't important. And I often miss the opportunities to worship the Savior in those moments of stillness.

I am still longing and looking forward. Only now, I look forward to better things. Easter Sunday with family and good friends, sure. Celebrations full of laughter, games, and maybe even some chocolate eggs — why not? But mostly I am hoping to better appreciate the significance of this sacred day.

This year as we plan our celebrations, may the significance of Easter not be lost on us or our families. May the day be filled with joy and sacred moments to be still and worship our risen Lord.

2: MEETING AND PASSING

But sanctify the Lord God in your hearts, and
always be ready to give a defense to everyone who
asks you a reason for the hope that is in you, with
meekness and fear.

(1 Peter 3:15)

A number of years ago in our former neighborhood, Greg and I had made a habit of doing a half-hour walk every day. As we walked, we would often notice the same older gentleman who was also out walking. One day we introduced ourselves. His name was Roy.

Roy was faithful to walk every day, and since it coincided with the time Greg and I liked to hit the sidewalks, we would frequently cross paths with him and stop to visit. We would speak briefly about the weather and what was going on in the neighborhood and then go our separate ways. It was a little like the Robert Frost poem, "Meeting and Passing":

> Afterward I went past what you had passed
> Before we met and you what I had passed.

As the weeks went by, however, we engaged Roy in conversations that went beyond the niceties. We asked him a little bit about himself. It turned out that Roy had become such a faithful walker because he had congestive heart failure. He told us that he was "living on borrowed time," that he was too old for a heart transplant, and there was nothing the doctors could do for him. So he walked every morning to save his life and to stay on his feet as long as he could.

Learning that, of course, we took an even greater interest in our neighbor. And we began to wonder out loud, "Do you think Roy knows Jesus?"

On subsequent walks we learned a bit more about Roy's story. He had been married to a woman who was a Christian Scientist and had divorced her. He really didn't believe in God or have much faith whatsoever. Little by little, we began to share about Jesus, about the changes He had made in our lives and the changes He could make in Roy's life, too. Roy seemed politely interested. Over the weeks, however, our conversations never seemed to progress beyond that point of initial, friendly interest.

Early one morning just before Easter, Greg and I were sitting at our kitchen table having devotions. Looking through our window, we saw Roy standing across the street. Because of his heart condition, he couldn't walk very quickly or for very long, and he would often pause to catch his breath before he continued on.

On that morning, he had paused right across the street from our window.

Greg and I had the same thought in that moment. Greg stood up and said, "That's it. Today is the day. I'm going to go out there and directly ask Roy what is keeping him from giving his life to the Lord."

I sat in the house and prayed while Greg walked across the street to talk to Roy. Toward the end of their conversation, Greg asked Roy if there was any reason he wouldn't give his life to Jesus Christ, who loved him and promised him eternal life and forgiveness of sins.

Roy said, no, he couldn't think of any reason not to do that. So he prayed with Greg right there on the sidewalk. Greg came back inside the house, absolutely beaming. He said, "Roy just gave his life to the Lord."

As the weeks went on, we continued our walks, regularly crossing paths with Roy. One time, with his face glowing, he said, "Well, you are looking at a new man because I have a new heart."

We knew immediately what he meant. He hadn't received a donor heart of flesh, but he had received something much more significant. Jesus had changed his heart and soul and had made him new on the inside. We were so excited because it was evident that faith had really taken root in our neighbor's life.

In another encounter on another day, he said, "You know, my heart hurts when I exert myself." Then he added, "But I was thinking about how much Jesus suffered for me and died for me. It makes the pain that I'm going through bearable."

On the way home we said to each other, "Praise God. He is meditating and drawing from the strength that the Lord has to offer him."

A short time after, we learned that Roy had passed into the presence of Jesus. It was sad, yes, to know we wouldn't see our fellow walker again on this earth, but we were so blessed that we'd had a part in helping him receive eternal salvation from the Lord. We knew we would be crossing paths with Roy in heaven.

But what if we had never spoken to him about Jesus? What if we had met and passed, met and passed, again and again, without ever saying anything beyond comments on the weather?

No, I haven't always seized such opportunities when they presented themselves. In fact, I'm sure I've walked right on by a great many open doors. How many other people have I met and passed, again and again, without ever speaking about my hope in Christ?

Looking back, I have often regretted my silence, but I have never regretted stepping out of my comfort zone to speak to someone about Jesus and salvation in His name.

3: SPEAKING UP

"If you keep quiet at a time like this, deliverance
and relief for the Jews will arise from some other
place, but you and your relatives will die. Who
knows if perhaps you were made queen for just
such a time as this?"

(ESTHER 4:14, NLT)

Do you like fairy tales?

I know my granddaughters do. It seems like every little
girl wants to be a princess. In one of my favorite stories from
the Bible, we find the account of a young girl who won a beauty
contest and ended up as the queen!

And it's no fairy tale.

In the Old Testament book of Esther, we read how the young
Jewish queen of the mighty Persian Empire risked her life to go
before the king and speak up for the lives of her people, the Jews,
who had been imperiled by a vast and hideous plot.

Mordecai, her older cousin and guardian, had strongly challenged her, saying,

"Don't think for a moment that because you're in the palace you will
escape when all other Jews are killed. If you keep quiet at a time like this,
deliverance and relief for the Jews will arise from some other place, but

you and your relatives will die. Who knows if perhaps you were made queen for just such a time as this?" (Esther 4:13-14, NLT)

So Esther stepped out of the comfort and apparent safety of her shelter in the queen's quarters and literally risked her position and her life to plead for her people, the Jews, who had been condemned to be exterminated by a certain high official in the empire. (It's a magnificent story! Get the whole context by reading this little book in your Bible.)

In the course of events in Esther, chapter 8, the young queen and Mordecai also found themselves in a place of unprecedented comfort and security. Their lives were no longer in danger from the ethnic cleansing and genocide of their enemies. The king had granted them authority and power, and they enjoyed amazing wealth, position, and access.

It might have been tempting at that time to just sit back and say, "We've come through the danger and achieved the security and safety that we needed." Esther was still queen, and Mordecai had been promoted to high office. What an amazing turn of events! But they knew that wasn't enough. Their fellow Jews across the empire were still in grave danger.

It wasn't time to kick back and relax on their royal pillows.

It was a time for action.

So it is in our lives. The Lord has us exactly where we are for a reason. We need to take every opportunity to speak up about our Lord, His salvation, and the hope of heaven whenever He gives us the opportunity.

4: FACE-TO-FACE WITH ETERNITY

Teach us to realize the brevity of life, so that we
may grow in wisdom.

(PSALM 90:12, NLT)

I just read about some crazy ways to celebrate New Year's Eve.
For some people, looking for the hottest party in town to count
down the new year seems too status quo. Instead, they want to
do something nutty, like skydiving out of a plane at midnight or
taking a plunge into the bone-chilling waters of Boston Harbor
or maybe joining more than 60,000 people in Venice's San
Marco Square who lock lips in the world's largest communal
kiss. Really?

Call me a killjoy, but I find myself with a reflective bent,
especially at the changing of the year. You might say that Woody
Allen and I have some things in common. He expressed this
outlook in one of his earlier films, *Hannah and Her Sisters*. Early
on in the film, there is some suspicion that he has a brain tumor.

"It's over. . . ." he panics. "I'm face-to-face with eternity. . . . Not later, but now! I'm so frightened I can't move,
speak, or breathe."

Just then, his doctor walks in with test results.

"Well, you're just fine. There's absolutely nothing here at
all."

When he finds out he's okay, he leaves the hospital. He's

running and jumping down the street, and then he stops. He realizes, *I'm not going to die from this brain tumor* now, *but I am going to die someday.*

It's been said that those who are prepared to die are most prepared to live.

So today I look back over the last twelve months and ask myself a few pointed questions.

If this weren't just the end of the year, but the end of my life, would I thank God for how I lived it?

- Did I grow in my understanding of who God is?
- Did I love Him more?
- Did I joyfully serve Him?
- Was I faithful in my relationships to my husband, children, friends, and ministry?
- Was I more attached to "stuff" that doesn't last?
- Was I more forgiving of those who hurt me?
- Was I a faithful steward with all that I am blessed with: my possessions, my health, my time?

Okay . . . it's good to be reflective now and then. But it's also good to celebrate!

Why? Because of the fact that we can take all our regrets to the Cross. Go celebrate the truth that forgiveness and a new beginning are promised to all who repent. Go celebrate the assurance that the Holy Spirit will continue to teach us, never leave us, and will see us through . . . for one more day, for one more year, and forever after that.

Yes, the end of our lives is one year closer. Which means we're one year closer to heaven.

5: SPARED FOR A REASON

Esther again pleaded with the king, falling at his feet and weeping. She begged him to put an end to the evil plan of Haman the Agagite, which he had devised against the Jews. Then the king extended the gold scepter to Esther and she arose and stood before him.

(ESTHER 8:3-4, NIV)

M y friend Shelley and I went on a bike ride not long ago and ended up at our favorite coffee shop. We sat down at a table with several other people and soon found ourselves in conversation with a shaken man who had just experienced a very close call. He had been driving his convertible on the freeway behind one of those trucks that transport multiple new cars. Suddenly, one of the cars in that trailer slipped from its perch, slid off the trailer, and flipped *over the top* of his convertible. It happened so fast that he hadn't even had time to react.

After he told us this, Shelley and I looked at each other and spoke the same words, almost simultaneously: "You have been spared for a reason. That was *God* who saved your life."

Just that quickly, it became very uncomfortable around that table.

As we biked on down the road, however, I felt peace about that brief encounter. It wasn't our responsibility to draw a response from those acquaintances or to persuade them to view events the way we did. Each of them had to make that decision for themselves. It was our responsibility to simply speak up about our faith. Would any of them remember that conversation and think about the brevity of life or a living God who might be more involved in their lives than they imagined?

Maybe, or maybe not. But Shelley and I hadn't missed the opportunity to speak up for Him, and for that I was happy.

The fact is, sometimes people will respond to our words about the Lord, and sometimes they won't. Whatever that response might be, we shouldn't let the fear of people or what they might be thinking keep us from sharing the good news of what God has done in our lives.

Going back to the story of Queen Esther for a moment, this young woman wasn't afraid to lose her dignity and wasn't ashamed to weep. She brought her deep concern, dropping to her knees and pouring out her heart before the king as she pleaded for her people. You and I need that same level of deep concern as we go before the Lord to plead for our friends, family, and neighbors who are outside of Christ.

Do you wake up at night thinking about your unsaved children? Does your heart ache for your unsaved parents, spouse, and relatives? Do you think about the people you pass in the street, realizing that many of them have "no hope and [are] without God in the world" (Ephesians 2:12)?

After I became a Christian, I remember being so excited about my faith. What an incredible secret of life I had just uncovered! I simply couldn't keep it inside. I went to school the next day, and in my first class I turned to the girl sitting behind me and said, "You won't believe what has happened to me! I have discovered the truth of the Bible and that Jesus has come into my life. I was searching for something: happiness, love, peace. All these things I wanted I found in a Someone! He has met the needs of my life. I feel like I've just got to tell you about this."

To this day I remember her reply. "Oh . . . well, I'm a Christian too."

I remember thinking, *You're a Christian too? You've known about this secret all along? You know Jesus? Every day in class I have sat in front of you, and you never mentioned it, never told me?*

Why wouldn't my classmate have taken the time to tell me about Jesus and salvation? I wanted so desperately to understand how that could be. As the years have gone by, however, I have come to understand how complacent, comfortable, and insulated we can become in our Christian culture. We forget what it was like *not* to know Jesus.

Are you reluctant to share your faith? Have you asked yourself why you're so reluctant?

Is it because you are afraid people might write you off as some sort of fanatic? That you will seem weird or out of touch? Maybe we need to balance that fear with the fear and reverence we have for God. We need to let Him burden our hearts to take that message to others, regardless of what they might think of us.

If someone wants to write you off as a fanatic, so be it. You and I are accountable to God, not to them. The truth is, however, I think many people will respect you for standing up for what you believe in if they know you are a believer. But if you let the conversation take its course and never have anything to share from your perspective as a person of faith, they may wonder how important that faith really is to you.

6: SOMETHING FISHY WITH OSCAR

All Scripture is given by inspiration of God, and is profitable for doctrine, for reproof, for correction, for instruction in righteousness, that the man of God may be complete, thoroughly equipped for every good work.

(2 TIMOTHY 3:16-17)

Oscar had a good life. He was a healthy, hearty fish, the size of a grown man's hand, and the boss of the entire aquarium. One by one, the other fish had to be rescued from his bad habit of nipping at their fins. Despite this aggressive behavior, the little boy* cared for him and fed him, along with a menagerie of other creatures: a bird named Popcorn, several snakes, and a favorite pet mouse.

Oscar's home was a comfortable aquarium that sat atop a chest of drawers in the boy's room. Every day after the boy went to school, Oscar would eye the empty room. He wasn't happy. How long had he been unhappy? Your guess is as good as mine. But this went on until one day the boy came home from school and discovered the aquarium empty! He panicked. Where on earth was that naughty fish?

Running to the chest to investigate, the boy found him stranded, gasping and gulping for air. Somehow Oscar had flipped himself out of the water, clearing the sides of the aquarium, and plopped helplessly in a bed of birdseed that had tipped over and spilled in the top drawer. There lay Oscar, covered in seeds, like he had just been breaded and was waiting to be fried and served up with a slice of lemon and some tartar sauce! The boy quickly grabbed him, ran to the tub faucet to rinse off the seeds, and then safely returned him to the little watery world where he belonged.

Cute story, but here's my point: Many times we define freedom as being free from any rules or restrictions that may hinder us. Most Americans identify with the attitude, "I'm the boss of me!"

But are we really?

Think of all the things that control you and your behavior. The list is endless. We are not truly free. What is it that you love and desire most of all? A beautiful body? A successful career? A house with a picket fence and two perfectly adorable children? You need to realize that if these are the things you live for, then no doubt they will limit your freedom.

Beautiful bodies demand that you'd better not eat that red velvet cupcake. And if you do, you'll feel guilty at best or stick your finger down your throat at worst.

A successful career will demand that you stay at your desk and finish the project due on Monday—even when your cousin from out of town is pleading with you to join her at the beach this weekend.

Those two adorable children will demand that you give up your svelte, prepregnancy figure, get up at night for feedings, change diapers, patiently attend to the unreasonable tantrums of a two-year-old, and remain in a constant mode of vigilance to keep them safe, healthy, and clean. (And guess who gets to paint the picket fence?)

All our choices are competing for control of our hearts. Even the "good" ones will make demands and place restrictions on our freedom. The key to true freedom is finding the right restrictions and making the right choices that fit our immortal souls.

All that we most love and cherish is already controlling us. The only question is, will we be under the control of the God of the universe, who can fulfill and satisfy us, or will we be under the control of some other lord who can't?

Here is where the Creator who designed us and loves us wants to come to the rescue. In the Bible, we have the guidelines and instructions for living to our Designer's specifications. We have Scriptures that are able to make us wise. Teaching, correction, and training are all clearly given to us in His Word (see 2 Timothy 3:16-17).

Submitting to the good and gracious "rules" that fit our immortal souls is the only way we will find true freedom. This is a great paradox: True freedom is in obedience. Freedom is found in following these rules, not in the release from them. If we foolishly disregard them, following our own hearts, we will end up violating our own being—much like Oscar the fish!

*By the way, that little boy was Greg.

7: BACKSTAGE PASS

Let us then approach the throne of grace with confidence, so that we may receive mercy and find grace to help us in our time of need.

(HEBREWS 4:16, NIV)

You and I have been given access to the throne of grace. While we are there, we need to speak to the Lord about people and ask for opportunities and boldness to give witness to our faith. I love that word *access*.

The truth is, I'm something of a groupie, and I love backstage passes and access badges. It's really fun for me when I go to an event and have the privilege of going behind the platform and seeing all the people participating.

One year at a Harvest Crusade, Greg sent a message to our eldest son, Christopher, telling him, "I left my Bible in the hotel room. I need you to go get it and come back quickly." So Christopher retrieved the Bible from the hotel, but then ran into a roadblock in his effort to get to the platform and give it to his dad. He didn't have the proper access badge. All he had was his dad's Bible. "I'm Greg Laurie's son," he told the security guard. "I need to get this to my dad. He called me, and I have his Bible."

The guard, however, wouldn't let him in. "No," he said. "You can't go in. This is as far as you can go. You don't have the proper credentials."

"But look," Christopher protested, "this is his *Bible*. See? It says so right here. It says 'Greg Laurie.' He called me and told me he needs it."

"Sorry," the man replied. "It doesn't matter that you have Greg Laurie's Bible. You don't have the proper credentials."

That's how the organizers have set up security at the crusades. One sort of badge will get you access to a certain point, and after that, you need another kind of access. And ultimate access allows you to go all the way onto the platform.

Well, there was Christopher with Greg's Bible. The crusade had already begun, and the music had started. Christopher knew he needed to get that Bible into his dad's hands.

"Look," he said, "I'm Greg Laurie's *son*. He's my *dad*, and he needs me." The man still wouldn't believe him until Christopher finally pulled out his driver's license and showed him the name and the photo. Finally the guard relented and allowed him the access he needed to get to the right room and hand the Bible to a very relieved Greg.

It amazes me to think that you and I, as followers of Jesus Christ, have instant access to the very throne room of God Himself. We can run right up to the throne of grace, to the very feet of the Almighty God who created and rules the universe. You may not have access to city hall or the governor's office or the White House, but you have *that* access. No angel, no matter how mighty or how holy, would dare bar the way and keep you from the King. God knows your name. You are His child. You can approach His throne of grace with any request at any time.

8: LEADING AND FOLLOWING

Imitate me, just as I also imitate Christ.

(1 Corinthians 11:1)

Britt and Rylie walked down the driveway, out to the car, the vintage red-and-white-checked cookbook in hand, a big smile on their faces.

"What are you girls up to?" I asked.

"We're going to the store to buy some ingredients for a recipe," Britt chirped.

"Oh, what a fun project on a summer day!"

"Look at this cookbook," Britt said. She flipped open the familiar, well-thumbed book to show me three names written, one above the other, on the inside cover. Carefully inscribed in large wobbly print were the names Molly, Brittni, and Rylie.

"This cookbook belonged to my mom," Brittni pointed out. "Here's where she wrote her name. Then I wrote mine, and now here is Rylie, too!"

"Brittni, that's so cool! Someday, Ry, you will put your daughter's name under yours!"

Three generations of young girls, one after the other, had turned the pages with their moms at their side, helping to choose just the right recipe for their appetites and abilities.

Molly followed her mom, Lee, and led Brittni, who followed her mom, Molly, and is now leading Rylie. It is a beautiful thing to realize that each day, in actions and words, we can lead generations by the good examples we set.

In the Scriptures, the apostle Paul wrote, "Imitate me, just as I also imitate Christ" (1 Corinthians 11:1).

In Brittni's case, her mom modeled a woman who loved her husband, her children, and most importantly, the Lord.

Let's be sure to choose our paths wisely, because each step we take is pointing the way for our children to follow.

One simple way to start our little ones on the path of righteousness is for each new mother to set aside time with her little ones to pray. Do you make time each day to model this important spiritual discipline?

If we would set aside this time (how long should be determined by the children's age and attention span), what a difference it would make. We could pray for friends and family by name, pray about the various crises and events we may have heard on the news, and pray for those who are suffering or sick. We could teach them to bring not only our private personal concerns, but the needs of loved ones, even strangers, before the Lord — enlarging their hearts.

Teaching our children to pray begins with making time for it. When is the best time for you and your family to pray together? After the morning news? After dinner? Before bed?

If each day we prayed with our families, leading them on the path, what a difference it would make in their day . . . and in their eternal perspective!

9: WHAT YOU HAVE TO LOSE

> Finally, they said to each other, "This is not right.
> This is a day of good news, and we aren't sharing it
> with anyone! If we wait until morning, some
> calamity will certainly fall upon us. Come on, let's
> go back and tell the people at the palace."
>
> (2 KINGS 7:9, NLT)

How big is your heart? How wide is your vision? Is it just for yourself, your immediate family, and a few friends? Is it just for brothers and sisters in the body of Christ? Or can you enlarge your heart and vision and concern for your entire neighborhood? For your state? For your nation? For the world?

In the Old Testament book of 2 Kings, we read about the city of Samaria, besieged by the Arameans, or Syrians, to the point that the people within the city walls were starving. It was so bad that a small measure of dove's dung was being sold for five pieces of silver. The famine in the city was so bad that this was the kind of thing people had to eat.

Then Elisha, the prophet of the Lord, gave this amazing prophecy: "Hear the word of the LORD. Thus says the LORD: 'Tomorrow about this time a [measure] of fine flour shall be sold for a shekel, and two [measures] of barley for a shekel, at the gate of Samaria'" (2 Kings 7:1). In other words, the famine would immediately end, and there would be great plenty. Overnight!

Suddenly a measure of fine flour would be sold for the normal, reasonable price. No amount of money could have purchased fine flour the day before.

At that time there were four men with leprosy who approached the entrance of the city. These guys were the outcasts of the outcasts. Nobody wanted anything to do with leprous men because not only was their condition horrifying to look at, it was contagious, and there was no cure.

The Bible allows us to tune in on the conversation these men had at the city gates:

> "Why should we sit here waiting to die?" they asked each other. "We will starve if we stay here, but with the famine in the city, we will starve if we go back there. So we might as well go out and surrender to the Aramean army. If they let us live, so much the better. But if they kill us, we would have died anyway." (2 Kings 7:3-4, NLT)

In other words, "What do we have to lose?"

So they went out to the camp of the enemy army, intending to surrender to them. When they arrived, however, no one was there! The camp was completely deserted. The four men went from one tent to another, eating the abandoned food, drinking the left-behind wine, and grabbing some of the valuables that were simply there for the taking. The Bible tells us that God had caused the Arameans to hear the sound of a great advancing army, and the soldiers fled for their lives, leaving everything behind.

After the four men had filled their stomachs and quenched their thirst, they began to experience qualms of conscience. After all, there were people just inside those city walls who were starving to death, and here they were with a king's feast set before them—more than they could eat.

Scripture records the scene with these words:

Finally, they said to each other, "This is not right. This is a day of good news, and we aren't sharing it with anyone! If we wait until morning, some calamity will certainly fall upon us. Come on, let's go back and tell the people at the palace."

So they went back to the city and told the gatekeepers what had happened. "We went out to the Aramean camp," they said, "and no one was there! The horses and donkeys were tethered and the tents were all in order, but there wasn't a single person around!" Then the gatekeepers shouted the news to the people in the palace. (2 Kings 7:9-11, NLT)

As a result, the city was saved just as the prophet had said it would be.

What a picture for today! Those of us who have found salvation in Christ have riches beyond imagination: the hope of eternal life in heaven, the forgiveness of sins, daily provision, the strength and wisdom of our Lord, and the comfort and guidance of the Holy Spirit. The book of Ephesians tells us that God the Father has *lavished* these things — the very riches of His grace — on those of us who are privileged to be called His sons and daughters.[1]

What will we do with those riches and all of that great abundance? Will we be content to simply enjoy it ourselves, while the world around us starves for a word of hope? If you do, here's what you lose: You miss out on sharing the greatest Good News story the world could ever hear. So share it with someone . . . today!

10: LITTLE LAMBS AND SCARY DREAMS

He said to him, "Tend My sheep."

(JOHN 21:16)

I t was late and dark when I heard the soft-but-not-quite-silent padding of small steps approaching on the carpet. Then I felt the small presence, paused at my side of the bed.

"Namma," she whispered, "I had a bad dream."

It wasn't a request, just a short statement of fact, and I knew what was needed. I threw back the covers and Rylie's night-gowned form slipped in. She snuggled closely and draped her slender arm around my waist. *Sweet,* I thought, *that she could come, without hesitation, like a little lamb, and find immediate comfort just being in my bed.*

As the years fly by, we mothers and grandmothers will remember and treasure the times when small troubles were so easily mended—when little lambs ran to us for safety and comfort. We are privileged to shepherd our little ones, leading them ultimately to our Great Shepherd.

Children are a lot like sheep. While every other animal under God's heaven can fend for itself (even a domesticated animal, when released into the wild, will discover survival instincts long forgotten), sheep can't. They can't hunt to find food, they can't fight to protect themselves, and they lack any homing sense to direct them to home and safety.

Your little flock needs to be observed carefully and receive abundant love and attention to thrive. You can't ignore or postpone their cries to a more convenient hour of the day, for mothering (or shepherding, for that matter) isn't the kind of job where you can clock in and out. You are on duty at all times, day and night, to care for your precious lambs.

What mothering requires is not only vigilance, but transparency. Kids can see right through the "do as I say, not as I do" lifestyle. If you hate vegetables and make sour faces every time you taste something green, do you honestly think your child will love to eat hers? By your daily life, you *show* them what God is like, even as you tell them about God, His Word, and His world.

This is big. Way big. It is the most important job you have. But don't feel alone in this role; we can find daily, moment-by-moment encouragement in God's promises—not in our own perfection. We need to know the Great Shepherd ourselves, and the task—simply defined—is to lead our little ones to *Him.*

So when the scary times come, the storms loom, or the wolves and bears threaten, we can trust them to the best Shepherd. When we are tempted to fret or be discouraged or take our loving concern and turn it into unproductive fear ("What if . . . ?"), we need to pray, "Lord, shepherd my flock! I will feed and tend and teach as You command me to, but please, I am depending on You to do what only You can. Bring each one safely to Your home, for I know You care for them even more than I do."

11: POSTCARDS WITH AN EDGE

Gently instruct those who oppose the truth.
Perhaps God will change those people's hearts, and
they will learn the truth.

(2 TIMOTHY 2:25, NLT)

How can we take what we know and make it understandable to the people who are close to us?

The apostle Paul gives us a big hint in 2 Timothy 2:24-25. He says, "A servant of the Lord must not quarrel but must be kind to everyone, be able to teach, and be patient with difficult people. Gently instruct those who oppose the truth. Perhaps God will change those people's hearts, and they will learn the truth" (NLT).

We are told not to strive or argue, but to be able to speak to everyone with gentleness, patience, and humility. As Paul said, "I have become all things to all men, that I might by all means save some" (1 Corinthians 9:22). He looked out at the people with whom he was trying to communicate and asked himself, "How can I take what I know is truth and present it to these people in a way they will understand it?" If you remember, he was once a Pharisee. I would imagine in his previous life, his idea of devotion to God was to look down his nose at anyone who failed to see things his way. But now Paul didn't want to be a stumbling block to those who were trying to understand the gospel message.

I like that phrase *by all means*. That says to me, "In every way I know how."

The church today has many means of communication at its disposal: TV, radio, print, the arts, music, drama, the Internet, social media, Twitter, and on and on it goes. All of these are simply vehicles for the timeless message of salvation in Jesus Christ. The bottom line for you and me is simply this: Let's get the Word out as quickly as we possibly can.

What means, as a woman, do you have today to reach out to the lost? It might be taking a plate of cookies to a neighbor and trying to build a bridge of friendship. All of us can find some way to reach out beyond ourselves with God's life-giving message of salvation and hope.

I remember one year when Greg was going to have a Harvest Crusade in Sydney, Australia. In the months prior to that outreach, our church in Southern California wrote postcards to hundreds and hundreds of addresses in Sydney, inviting people to the crusade. So the handwritten invitations arrived in these Australian homes, with a U.S. stamp. I have to imagine that many people at least gave them a second look!

What means do you have available? Some of the women in our church knit scarves to send over to Russian women along with gospel messages. You may not have the ability or opportunity to get up in front of a group to preach or to give out a message on radio or television, but you can reach someone in a creative way, demonstrating that the gospel is more than just words. It also can be backed up with tangible, practical deeds of kindness and compassion.

We never know when we may run out of opportunities to share the Good News with someone.

12: CATALOG WORLD

But the path of the just is like the shining sun, that
shines ever brighter unto the perfect day.

(PROVERBS 4:18)

I pick up the socks from the floor and rub the toothpaste off the
mirror. It's lunchtime, and I just finished cleaning up after
breakfast. The buzzer on the dryer goes off, reminding me
with every passing minute that laundry waits to be folded and
put away. When the phone rings and friends ask, "Are you busy?
What are you up to?" I shrink at the thought of another day
gone. *What in the world of significance have I done?*

"No," I may reply. "I'm not busy; I'm just cleaning up around
here."

I pick up the mail and flip through catalogs I don't remember subscribing to, but have somehow found their way into my
kitchen. In "catalog world," the women are forever twenty-five
years old. Houses are spotless with nothing needing repair, and
there's not a dish out of place. Plants never droop. Flowers never
fade. And most of the time, you will never see children — unless
they are quietly curled up in a cozy chair with a book in their
perfectly decorated rooms. Pillows remain fluffed and couches
unwrinkled.

Somehow we imagine life should be like this. Catalog world!
Some would like us to think that marriage and motherhood is a
job for those who otherwise couldn't find meaningful employment.

Being a homemaker is not a hobby. I didn't collect a husband, children, and now grandchildren because they are cuter than shoes. Homemaking isn't something I squeeze into my free time between going to the gym, getting my nails done, and shopping. It is something God has given me to do — twenty-four hours a day, seven days a week. It is my calling (my privilege!) to spend time and energy caring for my family.

You won't get this perspective from our contemporary culture. Watching sitcoms or reading romance novels won't inspire you to lay down your life for the sake of others or wisely use your precious limited resources.

I can only tell you what I know the Bible says clearly: *To find your life, you must lose it.* The greatest One in all the universe came and emptied Himself for our sakes and was given a name that is above every name. Only if we follow Him faithfully will we share in joy and life and glory that are unimaginable.

We Christian women must have a different paradigm. Evaluating people and things on a mere eighty or ninety years of life, instead of eternity, is a bad bargain. If you can only imagine the beauty of your simple life, shining ten billion years into eternity! The Word of God is crystal clear about the significance and reward of even a cup of water given in His name (see Mark 9:41). Jesus Himself notices and will reward the smallest good you do, even though others may not.

Are you living and loving and serving in a way that will shine ever brighter unto that perfect day (see Proverbs 4:18), or will what you do appear like a vapor of smoke, only to vanish away (see James 4:14)? Your outlook regarding these small, seemingly insignificant details is your revealing answer.

May we lift up our eyes and see, from our little rooms and this short hour, beyond all time and space to the Lord God of eternity. May we be among those faithful women who "by persistence in doing good seek glory, honor and immortality, [to whom] he will give eternal life" (Romans 2:7, NIV).

13: AN ERRAND TO RUN

Be very careful, then, how you live — not as unwise
but as wise, making the most of every opportunity,
because the days are evil.

(EPHESIANS 5:15-16, NIV)

Every now and then, I feel the nudge of God's Spirit urging me
not to procrastinate in reaching out to my neighbor, friend,
or family member who needs the Lord. We never know when
we may run out of opportunities to share the Good News with
that person.

Greg's cousin just had a heart transplant at the UCLA
Medical Center. We have seen this cousin over the years, but we
had never really sat down with him and said, "Are you a believer?
Do you know Jesus Christ as your Savior?" When we got word
that he was going in for transplant surgery, Greg made a trip up
to UCLA and came away with the assurance that his cousin
truly was a believer and had placed his life in God's hands.

On another occasion, Greg had a conversation with his
mother shortly before she died. There had never seemed to be an
opportunity for Greg to directly ask her one-on-one, "Are you
sure that you know Jesus? Are you sure that you will go to heaven
when you die?"

The day came when Greg felt very strongly that he needed to
speak to his mother about her relationship with Jesus. He went

over to her house and was pleased to learn that her husband, Bill, needed to go out and run an errand.

But then Bill changed his mind, saying, "I can run that errand later. I'll just stay here and visit with you." Greg knew, however, that as long as her husband was around, it was going to be very difficult for him to have a direct conversation with his mom. He knew that she would be distracted and reticent to talk about serious matters. That's when God gave Greg the boldness to say, "No, Bill. I will stay and talk to Mom. You go ahead and run those errands."

When Bill finally left, Greg was able to have the conversation with his mother that he had been wanting to have since he first became a believer.

You see, Greg also had an errand to run—from God Himself.

At one point he asked his mom point-blank if she had trusted Jesus Christ for her salvation. She replied, "I'm not comfortable with this conversation. I don't want to have this conversation right now."

Greg said kindly but firmly, "No, we *are* going to have this conversation."

And they did. It wasn't easy or comfortable, but they talked as never before about salvation in Christ and how to make sure of heaven. As Greg left, he sent up a silent prayer, "Lord, I don't know how effective that was. I just ask You to let it have an effect on Mom's life."

The next day, Greg's mom called the church office and asked, "What time are the services on Sunday?" And she came. As it turned out, it was the last time she was in church, and she passed away shortly thereafter. We are so thankful that Greg hadn't delayed or procrastinated that difficult conversation because his mother didn't have much time left on earth.

We, too, have limited time. We don't know when our friend's

or relative's last day will be. We don't know when *our* last day will be. We don't know when Jesus will return, calling His church home.

Let's seize the moment and do something about it, leaving the results up to God.

I want to close this chapter with a poem I read years ago and have never been able to forget. It's called, simply, "A Voice from Eternity":

> You lived next door to me for years
> We shared our dreams, our joys and tears.
> A friend to me you were indeed,
> A friend who helped me when in need.
>
> My faith in you was strong and sure;
> We had such trust as should endure.
> No spats between us ever rose,
> Our friends were like — and so, our foes.
>
> What sadness then, my friend, to find
> That after all, you weren't so kind
> The day my life on earth did end
> I found you weren't a faithful friend.
>
> For all those years we spent on earth
> You never talked of second birth.
> You never spoke of my lost soul
> And of the Christ who'd make me whole!
>
> I plead today from hell's cruel fire
> And tell you now my least desire —
> You cannot do a thing for me;
> No words today my bonds will free.

But, do not err, my friend, again —
Do all you can for souls of men.
Plead with them now quite earnestly
Lest they be cast in hell with me!

Let's make sure we take advantage of every opportunity we find to share our faith, using all of the care, creativity, kindness, and humility that God gives us.

14: "FORGIVE ME FOR MARRYING HIM!"

Most important of all, continue to show deep love
for each other, for love covers a multitude of sins.

(1 PETER 4:8, NLT)

I was eighteen, a new bride, full of myself, idealistic, and trying my best to be the perfect "Suzy Homemaker."

One morning, shortly after returning from our honeymoon, we had a doozy of an argument, the subject of which has long since been forgotten. Whatever it was, I felt I was right and he was definitely wrong. The argument dragged on until, in utter frustration, I blurted out, "I'm going to call my mother and tell her I want to go back home!"

Truth be told, I had no intention whatsoever of doing that. All I wanted was to get his attention and for him to see it my way and apologize. I wanted to win this one.

With Greg calmly looking on (this annoyed me even more), I picked up the phone and pretended to dial the number.

"Hello, Mommy," I said to no one, "I want to come home."

I went on pretending that she was answering me. But then . . . the phone started making those loud, rapid tones it makes when it's been left off the hook—and it was perfectly obvious what I was up to. Greg smiled, got up, and walked out of the room. I looked pretty ridiculous, but I still went on pouting the rest of the day.

Most of us can relate to how Ruth Graham felt shortly after she married Billy. They had had a little spat, and as he was driving off, she tearfully prayed, "Oh God, if You'll forgive me for marrying him, I'll never do it again!"

I can laugh at myself as I look back now, but at the time I was really upset. Today I can say without hesitation that I am happily married. But every relationship will have its conflicts. There's no such thing as a marriage made in heaven, but there is such a thing as a happy marriage that works—and at times, *work* will be the optimum word.

The apostle Peter deals with life so realistically in his first epistle (see 1 Peter 4:7-11). He assumes that various problems will occur in every human relationship. It's that way in every family, in every marriage. Even the first-century church had its share of divisions and arguments.

So when such things happen in our marriages, how are we supposed to go forward? Of course, we can't simply sweep things under the rug and ignore bad behavior. Wrongs will need to be confessed and apologized for in order for relationships to be restored. But here is the main point that Peter wants us to remember: "Love each other deeply, because love covers over a multitude of sins" (1 Peter 4:8, NIV).

Peter assumes, realistically, that sin and offenses will be committed. That's a fact. Period. But we must be prepared to forgive offenses and cover them over with love.

There is no way to undo what has been said or done, just as there is no way back to the innocence of Eden. Too often we coddle ourselves and cherish the wounds and scars, mulling over each miserable detail, nitpicking each word, glance, and tone of voice.

There is only one way forward: through the Cross, to forgiveness and forbearance. Let's love each other with love that is *muscular and strong*—the kind of love that can cover a multitude of sins.

C. S. Lewis once said,

It is perhaps not so hard to forgive a single great injury. But to forgive the incessant provocations of daily life — to keep on forgiving the bossy mother-in-law . . . the nagging wife, the selfish daughter, the deceitful son — how can we do it? Only, I think, by remembering where we stand, by meaning our words when we say in our prayers each night "Forgive us our trespasses as we forgive those that trespass against us." We are offered forgiveness on no other terms.[1]

Remember, sometimes the only way forward is through the Cross.

15: FRIED CHICKEN OR CARROT STICKS?

> Therefore, get rid of all moral filth and the evil that
> is so prevalent and humbly accept the word planted
> in you, which can save you.
>
> (JAMES 1:21, NIV)

We are to accept God's Word with genuine and heartfelt humility. It is the word of truth that introduces us to the living Word, Jesus Christ. James 1:18 tells us that as a result of being born again by responding to the word of truth, we believers become a kind of "firstfruits" in God's created order.

Firstfruits?

The term may not be familiar to twenty-first-century Americans, but James's mostly Jewish audience would have understood that concept right away. Firstfruits was one of the festivals the Jews were required to celebrate each year. At the time of harvest in early spring, they were to gather the firstfruits from their crops, vineyards, groves, and flocks and present them as an offering to the Lord.

In other words, these things were devoted to God. When I bring Him the first bushel of fruit from my trees, it's a symbol that the whole crop belongs to Him. When I bring Him the first lamb born to a ewe in my flock, it's a symbol that He really owns the whole flock—and everything else in my life too!

These firstfruits never were used for personal purposes.

They weren't kept, they weren't stored, and they weren't sold to anyone else for a profit. They belonged to God Himself.

When we think of our lives in that way, it's a strong reminder that we are not our own. Bottom line: *Our lives don't belong to us.* As Paul said in 1 Corinthians 6:19-20, "Don't you realize that your body is the temple of the Holy Spirit, who lives in you and was given to you by God? You do not belong to yourself, for God bought you with a high price. So you must honor God with your body" (NLT).

In other words, I no longer have the option of choosing to live the life that I would like to live. No, I must choose to live the way *God* wants me to live. I give up my right to determine the purpose, calling, and future of my life. I yield it over to God. It is devoted to God, He bought it with the blood of His own Son, and it belongs to Him.

How do we live in a way that pleases Him? We do it by humbling ourselves under the daily instruction and correction of the Word of God.

Do you have that kind of relationship with God through the Scriptures? When you open up your Bible, do you look at it and say, "Well, I like this part, but I don't care for this other part. I'm going to set that aside for now"?

God doesn't intend us to pick and choose from His Word as though it were a long buffet line. (I like the fried chicken and peach pie, but I can really do without the broccoli and carrot sticks.) Instead, we submit our lives to the teaching and exhortation of God's Word. *All of it.* As we flip through the pages of the Bible, we allow God's Spirit to use those truths to speak to various areas of our lives. We humble ourselves under it.

It won't always be easy!

In fact, by submitting to the Word of God, we set ourselves up for a head-on collision with our culture. Many in our society today might say, "Yes, the Bible is an excellent book, containing some good moral stories . . . along the line of Aesop's Fables. It's a book of advice, with some general counsel on how to love your families and how to be kind and good to people. But in reality our lives are our own. We are the ones who determine what we want to do. I am the captain of my ship. I am the master of my destiny. Living my life is really up to me."

In other words, if God's Word happens to align with my views and with my plans, then fine, I will accept it. But if, for instance, the Bible tells me that I ought to stay in a marriage when I would rather not or carry a baby to term when I would rather not, then my desires take precedence. In the end, it's up to me.

But that is *not* how it is meant to be for believers.

James called the Word of God "the perfect law." And it is perfect because the entire landscape of the Bible — poetry, history, narratives, stories, wisdom literature, prophesies, the accounts of Jesus' life, and the letters from the apostles — is relevant. They are *all* perfect. There is not one part of the Bible that is not applicable, in principle, to our lives. There aren't parts we can throw out because we don't like them. We should expose our hearts to the entire Word of God, even when we don't like what it's telling us or even when it takes aim at the sins we want to coddle.

Paul put it like this: "All Scripture is inspired by God and is useful to teach us what is true and to make us realize what is wrong in our lives. It corrects us when we are wrong and teaches us to do what is right" (2 Timothy 3:16, NLT).

We don't just read the Bible to hear things that make us feel better.

We humble ourselves under it.

We allow it to literally shape our lives.

16: WHEN IT'S TIME TO STOP TALKING

The earnest prayer of a righteous person has great
power and produces wonderful results.

(JAMES 5:16, NLT)

My husband, Greg, has often said, "Your loved ones may
escape your presence, but they can never escape your
prayers."

For a number of years, my devout Catholic mother prayed
for my sisters and me. She often sat us down on her bed and tried
her best to reach our hearts with words that, honestly, went in
one ear and out the other. This proved to be a great test of her
faith. Time after time, I mechanically nodded in outward agreement
while staring blankly out the window, wishing it would
end. I learned not to disagree or raise an objection, only because
it would have prolonged the torture.

I was utterly disinterested in what she was saying.

Then one day, it dawned on me. My mother had quit her
daily lectures. It was a relief; no more lengthy discussions at the
dinner table or in her bedroom. Whew! I had escaped her incessant
pleading!

I had escaped her pleading with me, but not her pleading
with God. It was much later, after I had come to faith, that she
revealed how she had determined to quit talking and instead to
diligently pray that her daughters would be saved.

I share this with you today and pray it will serve as an encouragement to you moms who have children who seem disinterested, even hostile to your faith. I know it may look hopeless at times, and you may be tempted to doubt that your prayers are being heard. But we need to know that when we pray for that lost child, we can have confidence those prayers are according to the will of God. *So keep seeking. Keep knocking. Keep asking.*

I often think of St. Augustine's mother, Monica. As a young man, Augustine cast off the faith of his childhood, but he could never cast off his mother's prayers and her stubborn love. They followed him from their small town to the big city of Carthage, where things in his life went from bad to worse. There, Augustine's life would be marked by what he later admitted were his "wicked ways" and "carnal corruption."

At twenty-nine, despite Monica's incessant pleading with him not to go, Augustine determined to set sail for Rome. Her prayer was that God would somehow prevent her son from making the journey. Despite her specific prayer that Augustine would not leave, he did, and she wept and wailed in sorrow. Although God didn't answer that specific request, He had heard the main point of her prayers. And He was at work in ways she couldn't see. In God's perfect plan and timing, so different from her own, the place she feared would be her son's undoing was the place he would finally surrender to God's will.

So may I challenge you who are weary and about to give up? *Don't.*

Though it may be a long wait, and it may seem like God is not at work, know that He is — in ways you can't always see.

17: THE BOOK YOU ARE WRITING

> If anyone among you thinks he is religious, and
> does not bridle his tongue but deceives his own
> heart, this one's religion is useless. Pure and
> undefiled religion before God and the Father is this:
> to visit orphans and widows in their trouble, and to
> keep oneself unspotted from the world.
>
> (JAMES 1:26-27)

We are all in some kind of spiritual shape. Dr. J. Vernon McGee once said that the only exercise some Christians get is jumping to conclusions, running down their friends, and sidestepping responsibility. Now that is *not* the kind of shape we want to be in. We want to be in good spiritual condition, and the Word of God will shape us.

James 1:26-27 gives us a three-part spiritual fitness test. We can test ourselves as to what kind of spiritual shape we are in and whether we are really being transformed by the Word of God. Some say that these two verses are a synopsis of the whole book of James.

Notice how James displays this fascinating balance between inner purity and outward actions. He is saying that a well-balanced, well-rounded Christian life will display *both*.

THE TEST OF THE TONGUE

The first test in verse 26 is to keep control of the tongue (or else your religion is essentially worthless). Some have said through the years that America's national pastime is baseball. I would say that it is *gossip*. There are more than 400 gossip magazines on sale on America's newsstands, and most of them are purchased by women.

Studies tell us that women speak twice as many words on any given day (some fifty thousand of them) as our male counterparts. Just to add a little perspective here, fifty thousand words is the content of a small- to average-sized *book*. Did you ever think about the fact that you utter enough words every day to fill the pages of a book? What sort of book are you writing with your speech?

Erma Bombeck said, "If I had my life to live over, I would have talked less and listened more." Wouldn't we all say that about our lives? More people have been killed by false, careless words than by the sword. Think about hateful dictators like Hitler, Stalin, Khomeini, and Ahmadinejad. These men may or may not have wielded a sword personally, but they certainly influenced others and brought about death and unspeakable destruction through their words.

Our words as women influence other women, our friends, our children, our husbands, our extended families, and our neighbors. The words we speak every day have an incredible, almost incalculable impact. Jesus Himself told us that we will one day give account before God for every idle or careless word that we have spoken (see Matthew 12:36). So that is one very large test as to whether or not we are being shaped by the Word of God: What sort of words do we speak on any given day?

THE TEST OF CARING

Verse 27 speaks about how we treat orphans and widows in their distress. These are the ones Jesus might have called "the least of these brothers of mine" (Matthew 25:40, NIV). We may find it relatively easy to use our gifts, our concern, and our talents to encourage and assist those whom we know and love, but the real test may lie in how we use our resources to help those in our community who are in the most desperate need.

In New Testament days, widows and orphans were the neediest segment of the church — and there were no safety nets, food stamps, food banks, welfare checks, or Salvation Army shelters to fill in the gaps. As I mentioned earlier, the early church came under tremendous persecution — so much so that those in Jerusalem had to flee their homes and neighborhoods for their very lives. Many others were martyred, leaving a large number of widows and orphans without support, protector, or provider. Some of these needy ones remained in Jerusalem because they had nowhere else to go, but many others were scattered across the Roman world. James was telling believers, "Wherever you are, whatever your circumstances, don't neglect these vulnerable people. Don't close your eyes to their plight."

Early societies such as the first-century church were structured around the family unit. Without a husband or a father, the family unit often fell apart. Widows and orphans found themselves without income, without guidance, and without care.

The church of Jesus Christ, then, was to become a large extended family for the most economically and socially vulnerable members of society. In the church, the "nobodies" were to be "somebodies."

In contemporary America, we may not often think of "widows and orphans" per se. But we still have many lonely, vulnerable, needy people in our midst. What about the elderly?

What about the unattractive? What about the sick? What about the uneducated? What about the single moms trying to hold things together and make ends meet? James is saying, "Don't shun or look down on or forget about those who need extra help in your world."

At one of our church's recent women's retreats, we heard Ellen Vaughn tell an interesting story about some seminary students at Princeton University. Their professor called them in and informed them that within a short time, they would be required to give an impromptu talk on the parable of the good Samaritan, to be delivered at an auditorium a few blocks away.

As the brief preparation period ended, the professor glanced at his watch and said, "Oh, by the way, we're running a bit late. You really need to get to the auditorium immediately."

As the seminary students poured out of the classroom building, they encountered another test they weren't even aware of. Directly in the path they had to walk to reach the auditorium, a man who had apparently been the victim of a violent mugging lay in the gutter. He had been made up to look beaten and bloodied and was seemingly unconscious. Many of these seminary students had to literally *step over* this man in their rush to get to the auditorium and deliver their messages on the parable of the good Samaritan.

Keep in mind, these students were intending to spend the rest of their lives in some kind of ministry. Yet something was painfully evident as they ignored the fallen man and rushed to complete their assignment: There was a huge disconnect between what they professed to believe and were convinced they believed and their response to a real-life situation at their very feet.

James tells us that what we *say* we believe and actually practice in daily life have to come together.

THE TEST OF PURITY

I love white linen. It is very beautiful but also very impractical. Why impractical? Because it's so difficult to keep clean. The minute you put it on, you invariably spill something on it. Or you sit down and make it creased and wrinkled. There's one thing about wearing white: You can immediately tell if you've soiled it or spilled something on it. James is saying that we are to be spotless in our inner purity, those places in our lives where no one else but Jesus can see.

In verse 27 we read the words "to keep oneself from being polluted by the world" (NIV). Not only are we to be pure in speech and concern ourselves with the weak and disenfranchised among us, but the third and final test is to keep ourselves from being stained, blemished, or spotted by the world around us. In other words, are we being shaped by the Word of God or by the culture in which we live?

It reminds me of Paul's exhortation in Romans 12:2: "Don't let the world around you squeeze you into its own mould, but let God re-mould your minds from within, so that you may prove in practice that the plan of God for you is good, meets all his demands and moves towards the goal of true maturity" (PH).

James is addressing not only our outward behavior here, but also the unseen areas of the heart, mind, and imagination. Even in *those* places, he tells us, we are to be pure, spotless, and unpolluted by the world.

The book of Ephesians tells us that Jesus Christ loved the church and "gave Himself for her . . . that He might present her to Himself a glorious church, not having spot or wrinkle or any such thing, but that she should be holy and without blemish" (5:25,27). In Revelation 19:7-8, we're told that "his bride has prepared herself. She has been given the finest of pure white linen to wear" (NLT).

Obviously, none of us can be completely, perfectly spotless. That is why the Bible says we are to be washed daily in the Word of God and by the blood of the Lamb. So yes, He cleanses us and forgives us. The apostle John writes that He will "[*continuously*] cleanse us from all unrighteousness" (1 John 1:9, AMP, emphasis added). But there is something for us to do as well. James is telling us to avoid any kind of immorality and to keep ourselves (as best we can) from the pollution and stains of this world.

Some of us are like St. Augustine, who prayed, "Lord, give me chastity . . . but not yet."

Within our churches there are Christians who engage in casual sex and live undisciplined, immoral lives. They use pornography, live together outside of marriage, and engage in extramarital affairs. It's not all that uncommon! In fact, there is often a huge disparity between what the Word of God is telling us and how we actually live our lives.

James is saying this ought not to be so. If your religion is true and not false, and if you aren't simply posing as a Christian, then your life should be one of spotless integrity. That means we will be very careful about how we walk in this world. We will make every effort to avoid immorality — and it won't always be easy! When we stumble and fall (as we inevitably will), we will confront the sin in our life, run to Christ for forgiveness and restoration, and seek God's help and strength to turn away from that sin and walk in a way that pleases the Lord.

18: WHAT GOD REALLY EXPECTS OF YOU

> To me, though I am the very least of all the saints,
> this grace was given, to preach to the Gentiles the
> unsearchable riches of Christ.
>
> (EPHESIANS 3:8, ESV)

Our riches in Christ!

We read the verse above and, because it may be familiar to us, we can breeze right over it. Just reading those words should be enough to thrill our hearts.

Our riches.

Yes, they really are ours!

And they truly can be possessed because they are given by the only One in the universe to whom all good and lasting things belong. He alone has the power to make such promises.

The God of all the universe has placed riches in the hands of every trembling believer — young and old — whether brand-new and just breaking in their gospel shoes on the road of life or a seasoned and wise traveler. These are the precious riches we could never in a million or billion years deserve. And because of His unmerited favor to us in Christ, they are ours!

But we so often feel that we are undeserving; we disappoint ourselves, not to mention others. So how do we know this promise of riches is true? And how do we use them?

I remember our dear friend Alan Redpath once asking, "Do

you know what God expects of you?" Immediately my mind went to the Ten Commandments and the contents of the Sermon on the Mount. But before I began to sink beneath the weight of my own guilty conscience, he said (with a grin, I might add), "He expects nothing from you but failure."

Sigh . . . it's true. We are, apart from His power and work in our lives, simply failures. Yet when we come empty-handed to His cross, trusting in His grace, we find our lives bound up in the bundle of His everlasting life—my sin for His blameless record, my guilt for His acceptance, my spiritual poverty for His boundless wealth.

If you aren't yet shouting, "Glory!" you should!

Meditating on a phrase like this one is like climbing the Alps of the New Testament. We are told that in Christ are unfathomable riches. The word in the Greek means "past finding out, not to be tracked out, unsearchable." The idea is that in Christ, our blessings are "too deep to be measured." The books of Ephesians and Colossians contain truths that can energize and invigorate even the most discouraged and doubting among us.

Often on sleepless nights, when I am awakened by troubling thoughts or fears, I have gone through these passages that I have committed to memory. How can I fear if I am so loved? How can I be lonely when I am His child? How can I condemn myself if I have been reconciled and forgiven? Sweet friends, I want to share the good news contained in these amazing passages with every struggling believer I can.

If we understand the fullness of our salvation that was accomplished at Calvary's cross, we will see our day-to-day lives transformed. Climb with me through these alpine meadows, breathe in the bracing air of these truths, and you will gain the perspective you need.

Before you can hope to have a fulfilling Christian life, family, marriage, friendship, ministry . . . before you find the buoyancy needed to stay afloat in times of crisis . . . before you can defeat those flaming arrows of doubt, you need to understand deeply, meditate on, and rub into your heart these great truths. Use them as spiritual and emotional resources. They are at your disposal, waiting to be put to the test!

Just think of these words that describe your position in Christ and what you already have because you've put your faith in Him. Say these words out loud for all to hear:

I am chosen, loved, reconciled.
I am forgiven, an heir, accepted.
I have redemption, hope, grace.
I am a citizen, adopted, sealed.

Explore, discover, and luxuriate in (imagine this like warm oil being rubbed into the dry, wounded, or calloused parts of your soul) these unfathomable treasures, and you will be transformed. Dear one, if you do this, you will know by experience the depth of God's great love for you in Christ Jesus.

Join me and say, "Oh, the depth of the riches both of the wisdom and knowledge of God! How unsearchable are His judgments and His ways past finding out!" (Romans 11:33).

19: MIRROR, MIRROR

Anyone who listens to the word but does not do what it says is like a man who looks at his face in a mirror and, after looking at himself, goes away and immediately forgets what he looks like. But the man who looks intently into the perfect law that gives freedom, and continues to do this, not forgetting what he has heard, but doing it—he will be blessed in what he does.

(JAMES 1:23-25, NIV)

M irror, mirror on the wall, who's the fairest of them all?"

So asked the wicked queen in the story of Snow White and the seven dwarves. She didn't like what that mirror had to tell her, and in the same way, we don't always like what the mirror of God's Word has to say, either.

James says we are to look into that mirror of the Word of God *intently.*

In that day, people didn't have glass mirrors. They used hand mirrors made out of highly polished metal. It wasn't the clearest image, perhaps, but they could see themselves a little bit in the reflection. That's what a mirror is all about: You see yourself in it. James is saying that when you look at the Word of God, when you look into the perfect law, you not only see history, stories, teaching, and counsel, but you see *yourself.*

We are to use the Word like a mirror.

That means we will study the Scriptures with determination to understand what God is saying to us. This isn't a casual glance over the page, as though we were reading a novel or a newspaper. No, James is speaking here of a serious, dedicated consideration of the words before us.

Here is something interesting: The Greek word James uses for "intently" in this passage is the very same word used to describe Peter and the way he looked into the empty tomb on Easter Sunday morning. I find that fascinating. Can you imagine Peter's reaction when he saw that stone rolled aside and an empty grave before him? He must have stared as though his eyes would pop out of his head. It was (to that point) probably the most amazing thing he had ever seen, and his mind was seeking to process the implications of what his eyes were telling him. He looked *intently* at that empty tomb, realizing that, one way or another, what he was seeing in that moment would change his life forever.

That is how we are to look at the Word of God. Do you read the Bible the way Peter looked into the empty tomb? How regularly? How carefully? Do you see each word? Each verse? Each chapter? Peter looked intently, and James says that is how we are to read God's Word.

Take time to consider: *What is this saying to me? How do these words impact my life today?* The fact is, if the Word of God is going to transform you, it has to be very personal to you.

The Bible isn't simply a textbook or a handbook or an instruction manual. It is a very personal message from God crafted just for you, at any and every given moment in your life.

The Word of God will show you who you are.

Maybe you have never read your Bible in this way. That doesn't matter; you can begin today. And when you look at the Word of God at this deeper level, it will certainly begin to speak to you . . . counsel you . . . correct you . . . comfort you . . . encourage you . . . and guide your steps.

I heard about a professor at an Ivy League school. When he was a young man, he decided to compile a book of all the things that had inspired him, helped him, or instructed him in the course of his life. Every time he read or heard a pithy thought, a clever quote, or an interesting turn of philosophy, he wrote it down in his book. He was amassing what he thought would be a volume that would talk to him, counsel him, and be everything he needed for his life. After many years of collecting and amassing this material, he had it all in front of him in a book of sorts. Sitting down under a tree on a summer's day, he opened up this book and began to read.

But he was disappointed. The words didn't really mean much to him or even make much sense to him *because his life had changed*. What had once moved him no longer moved him. What had once spoken to him no longer spoke to him. What had once seemed so profound now rang hollow in his ears. It was just a mishmash, a random scrapbook, and it didn't help him at all.

Later in life when he had become a Christian and encountered the living Word of God, he said, "I have found the Book I have been looking for." It spoke to him. It spoke to him in fresh ways each day. It *continuously* spoke to him. It spoke to him no matter what his circumstances were or how his situation had changed.

Has that happened to you? Has the Bible shown you who you are better than any counselor ever could? Look intently into its pages, asking God's Holy Spirit for insight and understanding.

Look as if you were looking into a mirror to discover things about yourself.

You will.

What's more, you'll discover (all over again) how deeply you are loved.

As Martin Luther wrote, "The Bible is alive, it speaks to me; it has feet, it runs after me; it has hands, it lays hold of me."[1]

20: SMALL PRAYERS

Don't worry about anything; instead, pray about everything. Tell God what you need, and thank him for all he has done.

(PHILIPPIANS 4:6, NLT)

D ear Jesus, please help Aunt Brittni find her glasses."

Three-year-old Lucy had been occupied with setting up her dollhouse in my family room when something (or should I say Someone?) prompted me to ask her to pause for a moment and pray with me for Brittni's lost sunglasses.

Brittni was upset because not only were the glasses new, they were *expensive*—her big birthday present that Jonathan had given her just two weeks before.

With our heads bowed, and with Dora the Explorer and her pals Diego and Boots silently looking on, we asked the Creator of the universe to graciously hear what to some may have seemed like an insignificant request.

That evening, Greg and I were out to dinner with some friends when the answer to Lucy's and my prayer came via a text from Brittni: "I found my glasses. . . . Jonathan had forgotten he had put them behind the visor in his car for safekeeping!"

Just a few months ago, I was the prayer director for Harvest America, a nationwide evangelistic outreach. Much prayer had been offered on behalf of all those who were inviting their loved ones to hear the gospel simulcast from Angel Stadium to more than 2,400 venues across the United States. What happened exceeded our expectations as tens of thousands of commitments were registered for Christ!

I wonder how it is that God not only hears and graciously answers the "big prayers," like those for Harvest America, but also simple, ordinary requests for lost glasses. Not only does He hear those small prayers, but He *delights* in them.

I am amazed when I consider the mind-blowing miracles Jesus performed while He was on this earth. One in particular touches my heart, the cry of a man with leprosy: "Lord, if You are willing, You can make me clean" (Matthew 8:2).

And with a loving touch Jesus replies, "I am willing; be cleansed" (verse 3).

"Lord, if You are willing . . ." This applies to all our requests. We don't know how the Lord may choose to answer a prayer for a nation, the salvation of a soul, or help finding lost sunglasses. (I can only imagine the angels must smile at such small requests.) But I do know this: I have learned there is no request too big or too small for Him to hear. He delights and welcomes them. Never once does He say, "Not now, I'm too busy!"

I read a poem by John Newton recently that may prove helpful in reminding ourselves whenever we hesitate in praying big or small prayers:

> Thou art coming to a King
> Large petitions with Thee bring;
> For His grace and pow'r are such,
> None can ever ask too much.[1]

Or too little!

As Dwight L. Moody once said, "Next to the wonder of seeing my Savior will be, I think, the wonder that I made so little use of the power of prayer."

21: IN THE SULTAN'S HOME

But the man who looks intently into the perfect law
that gives freedom, and continues to do this, not
forgetting what he has heard, but doing it — he will
be blessed in what he does.

(JAMES 1:25, NIV)

As a young girl I lived in Kuala Lumpur, Malaysia. When I
was about eleven or twelve years old, I was invited by a girlfriend to spend a week with her at a retreat in the mountains
called the Cameron Highlands. My friend's family car drove us
through a lush, beautiful jungle as we wound our way upward
into the hills. At the top of the highlands was a beautiful home
that was actually a sultan's home.

We spent a week in this amazing palace, high above the hot
and muggy lowlands. We were actually high enough in elevation
that it grew chilly and misty in the mornings and nights. It felt
wonderful.

Seemingly every room in the house had a fireplace, and in
the chilly evenings the servants would build fires. Then one
evening my girlfriend and I foolishly decided we would build a
fire ourselves. But what would we burn in the fireplace? I'm
ashamed to even tell you what we did.

Bookshelves graced many of the rooms in this mansion, and
the sultan had a marvelous collection of books and glossy magazines. We were such silly girls! Instead of calling for someone to
help build a fire for us, we actually took some of the books and

magazines and began tearing out pages to use as kindling. We built our own fire and reduced a number of those books and magazines to ashes.

Yes, I suppose we had been free to take those gorgeous books and misuse them. But what a shame to destroy them the way we did! How much more glorious it would have been to take those books, open them up, and actually *read* them. We might have had some marvelous adventures as we explored strange and wonderful places and learned of people we would never meet in our lifetimes. Instead, all we had left that next morning was a pile of cold ashes.

In the same way, we are free to take these lives of ours and use them as we wish. If you want to disregard the laws of God (and don't run afoul of civil laws), you can do that. You can use up your life just as I took the pages of those gorgeous books and burned them up for a temporary surge of warmth and a little flame that extinguished so quickly.

How much better to use our lives the way that God intends for us to use them. The perfect law James speaks of is a matchless, incomparable manual for life itself. We take our lives and humble them under the instructive Word of God. We allow it to speak to us, to shape us, to instruct us. We deliberately align ourselves with the Word as we seek to discover God's design, desires, and plans for each one of us.

As a result, we refuse to commit adultery, steal, lie, or cheat because that would break the laws of God, hurting Him, hurting others, and hurting ourselves. When God says to take care of our neighbor, we look for ways to do that. When He says to love our spouse and children, we seek His help to do that to the best of our ability. As the apostle Paul says in Ephesians 5:10, we "find out what pleases the Lord" (NIV).

We realize our full potential only as we apply this marvelous, heaven-sent care manual to our lives.

22: SNAP, EDIT, POST

He made us accepted in the Beloved.

(EPHESIANS 1:6)

'm a people-pleaser.

I confess it.

For years I found a way to excuse this flaw by thinking, *Of course I want to please everyone. After all, I was a middle child* (as if my birth order would somehow exempt me from a hole in my character).

Of course I want to be good. But too often I want to be liked even more. Can you identify with me on this? Isn't that why we post only the attractive pictures of ourselves, or pictures with people we admire, or better yet — a celebrity? It is one way to say, "Would you please like me? After all, look! I'm hanging out with these fun, important, beautiful people!"

And as for those other photos that don't make us look good, we can simply edit or delete or forget them altogether by boxing them up next to old Christmas ornaments in the garage.

In the old days, people could size others up by whom they married, who their parents were, or what they did. Now, through the ease of social media outlets, we can easily edit our lives to make us look great. We present to the world of "friends" *our good side* . . . and hopefully they will like us.

I use Facebook and Instagram because I enjoy seeing what

my friends and family are up to. I like to post articles and thoughts I have about what I am doing or reading. But the truth is, sometimes all this tempts me to paint and present my humdrum, rather ordinary life as more happy, beautiful, and exciting than it is. How often do we find a post where someone is asking for forgiveness, confessing their mess-ups, or posting an unattractive photo of themselves? Rarely.

Maybe this is the Holy Spirit talking just to me. But I don't think so. May God give us the courage to face the unattractive sides of our lives and welcome His perspective on who it is that we really are.

Are we truly the people in the photos, caught in that soft lighting, smiling broadly at the camera? *Sometimes.* But more often, we are not. Have you ever used your iPhone to take a picture and hit the reverse camera feature that reverses the lens to display not the subject you had in mind but yourself instead? Startling, isn't it? Is that the real you, the real me, staring back? (Or in my case, squinting at the lens like a mole?) There we are, caught off guard in stark, unedited, unsettling reality.

That's why I am continually amazed that God calls us His friends. If there were a heavenly Facebook somewhere and I were God, I would have left me in "friend request" limbo. And yet, by the greatest display of love ever, I have made it onto His "Friends" list.

He sees exactly who we are, right down to the essence of our self-absorbed beings. And yet He still loves us. That's grace. As Anne Lamott said, "I do not at all understand the mystery of grace — only that it meets us where we are but does not leave us where it found us."[1]

Because of the saving life of Christ, we are accepted in the Beloved (see Ephesians 1:6), friends of God. How amazing is that?

So what do we do with such an undeserved gift of love and acceptance?

- Receive it and use it to see the truth about who we are.
- Repent daily (or more often!) from merely trying to look good.
- Refocus our desires from pleasing others to pleasing God.

After all, who really cares about you more?

23: THE POWER OF NEW LIFE

"I am the vine, you are the branches. He who
abides in Me, and I in him, bears much fruit; for
without Me you can do nothing."

(JOHN 15:5)

Every autumn, the deciduous trees shed their leaves in a shower
of glory.

But maybe not all of them.

Sometimes a few leaves cling to the branches, as if unwilling
to accept the inevitable and drift to the ground. A good wind
may remove what leaves remain . . . but again, not all of them.
Some of those old leaves, brown and withered as they might be,
keep clinging right through autumn and on into winter.

Then comes spring, and that dawning season finally takes
care of any leaves the winds have left behind. How does spring
do it? *With the power of life.* As the sap rises and new life flows
through the trunk and branches of the tree, the baby leaves push
the old clinging leaves off the tree, sending them on their way at
last.

It is the old (finally) giving way to the new.

Thomas Chalmers, a Scottish pastor and teacher from the
1700s, wrote an article that spoke of "the expulsive power of new
affections."

I love that word *expulsion*. I looked it up in my dictionary and discovered that it means "driving, forcing, ejecting, banishing, pushing, or exercising." I picture it as the force of life—the very life of Jesus Christ within us—pushing away those old addictions, attachments, and dead things that tend to cling to our branches.

It's really all about falling in love with Jesus. When we truly fall in love with Him, we find ourselves able to reprioritize our lives.

If you are married, do you remember how you forgot your old affections and attachments when you found the true love of your life? It was easy, wasn't it? It wasn't hard to give up those things at all. In fact, it happened almost instantaneously.

All of us need to recheck our priorities from week to week and day to day. Sometimes we may sense the Lord's prompting us to let go of something, but we don't want to let go *right then*. We want to hold on to it for a little while. As a result, we find it difficult to make any progress in our Christian lives. It's simply because we're not willing to lay aside that sin or distraction or momentary pleasure to fulfill our deepest need: to become conformed to our Lord and be daily changed into His likeness.

This past summer I had the opportunity to bring a woman to a Harvest Crusade, where she gave her life to Christ. Since then, a friend and I have met with her a couple of times in an effort to help her become grounded in the Lord. Though she definitely wants Jesus in her life and sees in my friend and me the characteristics and fruit that come as a result of a life of walking with Jesus, loving Jesus, and raising our kids for Jesus, she is having trouble making any headway. She truly wants the fruits of the Christian life but is so entangled by her old lifestyle and relationships that she seems almost immobilized. She wants to get to church, read her Bible, and meet with other believers, but never seems able to "find the time."

The fact is, unless she becomes willing to make Jesus her

first priority, all of the things she saw as so attractive about the Christian life never will become a reality for her.

Life flows from Christ, the Vine, and from Him alone.

Just wishing for fruit never will put it on the branches.

24: SPIRITUAL SHAMELESSNESS

But your iniquities have separated you from your
God; and your sins have hidden His face from you,
so that He will not hear.

(ISAIAH 59:2)

once knew a woman whose husband had been cheating on her
for years.

She had no idea. One day, however, the whole sordid thing
came to life in a shattering, deeply painful way. All those birthday presents, valentines, Christmas gifts . . . what did they really
mean now? Lie upon lie, so much deception. Now she knew the
truth, that his heart was given to another. Finally, when it all
came to light (as these things eventually will), he "came clean,"
asking for her forgiveness. The good news about this story is
that, in a supreme act of grace, she gave him another chance. It
took many years, however, to heal both of them.

It is tragic to hear a story like this one. But don't imagine that
it is any less tragic when we are habitually unfaithful to God.

I don't think God likes it when we saunter back into His presence, casually thinking that He will always overlook our sin. This
was true in the case of the nation of Israel, in Jeremiah's day. They
had gone "whoring" (God's words, not mine; check out the entire
book of Hosea), and now they came back to the Lord, noncha-
lantly saying, "My Father, my friend from my youth, will you

always be angry?" (Jeremiah 3:4-5, NIV).

It would be like an unfaithful spouse bringing candy and flowers home after a day of cheating. Keep your candy and flowers, and just stop the cheating!

The Israelites had offended God, and He had seen right through the pretense of their shallow confessions. He states calmly—and sadly, "This is how you talk, but you do all the evil you can" (verse 5, NIV).

Sin's subtle deception is perpetrated on *our own hearts.* All the pretty fantasies and religious words we say mean nothing to God if, in our hearts, we continue to cherish and hide ungodly behavior.

We may fool others, and most likely we are trying to fool ourselves. But God is not convinced. Today, let's "come clean" and label our sin (whatever form it takes) for what it is. I challenge you to use the old-fashioned biblical words for sin when you confess to God: thief, drunkard, fornicator, idolater, glutton, sloth . . . Shocking, I know, but we need to be shocked by our heart's capacity to sin.

So let's stop all the pretense and self-deception. Don't think nostalgically that because you once had a vibrant relationship with the Lord, it will somehow compensate for your present coldness and disregard for sin.

Hear what God says: "I am merciful. . . . I will not be angry forever" (verse 12, NIV). But first, you must "return . . . acknowledge your guilt—[that] you have rebelled . . . and have not obeyed" (verses 12–13, NIV).

May God remove the blindness we have to our own sin so we can truly rejoice in His love and forgiveness.

Lord, help me to search my heart, and see if I have taken advantage of Your grace and mercy. Convict me of my sins, however big or small they may be in my eyes. Help me see how I have offended You. Resensitize my conscience, and help me forsake evil altogether. Have mercy on me and give me a humble and contrite heart.

25: WHAT TO DO WITH TEARS AND FEARS

In the morning, O LORD, you hear my voice; in the morning I lay my requests before you and wait in expectation.

(PSALM 5:3, NIV)

I have watched seven babies come into the world. Two were my own sons, one was my sister's son, and four were my grandchildren. One thing has been consistent through each unique and marvelous experience: They all came out crying.

The first sounds we make as infants are cries. I doubt very much that these tears are tears of sorrow; babies are not experienced enough to know sadness. But they do understand fear. Don't you wonder what they're thinking about in their little minds?

What's happening to me? It's much colder, much louder . . . and what's grabbing and moving me all around? Whaaaaa! I want my private, warm, and safe room back!

Tears and fears—that's the way we come into the world. From our first breath to our last, we should expect them.

That is one of the most striking features in the unique book of Psalms. I have come to appreciate how deeply emotional they are. Most of us like to think that we are honest about our emotions, but really, when you read the Psalms, don't you have to wonder if we have ever been *this* honest in our own prayers?

Listen to one psalmist's cry:

> I am worn out from groaning;
>> all night long I flood my bed with weeping
>> and drench my couch with tears.
> My eyes grow weak with sorrow;
>> they fail because of all my foes.
>
> Away from me, all you who do evil,
>> for the Lord has heard my weeping.
> The Lord has heard my cry for mercy;
>> the Lord accepts my prayer. (Psalm 6:6-9, NIV)

These ancient poems are full of sighs and cries to the God who hears. In these wonderful prayers and songs written so long ago, we have the full spectrum of emotions we human beings could experience. But don't lose sight for a single moment that the Psalms are inspired Scripture. It is as though we are being given permission to speak this honestly to a God who cares. As a matter of fact, if you were to take all 150 psalms and break them into categories, you would find there are more psalms classified as psalms of lamentation than any other. The biggest piece of the psalter are tears and fears.

Yet still, sometimes Christians believe a little myth, and the myth goes like this: *If I am a good little girl, God will not let anything bad ever happen to me.* Now if you read your Bible at all (and you are careful not to pick and choose only pleasant passages), you would realize this naive thinking is nowhere in the canon of Scripture.

The thing we need to realize is that though life is full of problems, God has promised to deliver us out of them all. Psalm 34:18-19 says, "The Lord is near to the brokenhearted and saves the crushed in spirit. Many are the afflictions of the righteous, but the LORD delivers him out of them all" (ESV). When you study the life of King David—and especially his words in the Psalms—there was hardly a time when he wasn't, in one way or another, engulfed in tears and fears.

It seems to me that when the Lord comes into a person's life, their heart actually becomes *more* vulnerable, *more* sensitive to pain and hurt. Believe me, I wish this weren't so, but it is true! One of my favorite children's stories is *The Velveteen Rabbit* by Margery Williams. Within its pages is a conversation on Christmas day between the Velveteen Rabbit and the much older and wiser Skin Horse. When the Velveteen Rabbit asks what is real, the Skin Horse patiently explains that it is a gradual process:

> "It doesn't happen all at once," said the Skin Horse. "You become. It takes a long time. That's why it doesn't happen often to people who break easily, or have sharp edges, or who have to be carefully kept. Generally, by the time you are Real, most of your hair has been loved off, and your eyes drop out and you get loose in the joints and very shabby. But these things don't matter at all, because once you are Real you can't be ugly, except to people who don't understand."[1]

Have you ever noticed that great saints are often great sufferers? For starters, you could take the greatest human heart that ever lived, Jesus Christ, as the best example. The book of Hebrews tells us that "during the days of Jesus' life on earth, he offered up prayers and petitions with loud cries and tears to the one who could save him from death, and he was heard because of his reverent submission" (Hebrews 5:7, NIV).

So what do we do with our tears and fears? Expect them. And then, pray them.

In Psalm 5, David was surrounded by enemies. Trouble loomed. And we can learn from him how to pray. He prayed,

> Give ear to my words, O Lord,
>> consider my sighing.
> Listen to my cry for help,
>> my King and my God,
>> for to you I pray.
> In the morning, O Lord, you hear my voice;
>> in the morning I lay my requests before you
>> and wait in expectation. (verses 1-3, niv)

Like David, we ought to deal with emotions by praying them honestly before God. Remember, He is not easily shocked; He sees you in the context of your entire life, not just in this given moment of pain. So tell Him how you feel. We have a God who listens and answers prayers.

Here are some points that stand out about David and his prayer.

There is a growing clarity. First, he sighs, moans (that is the meaning of the Hebrew word sometimes translated *meditation*, verse 1), then he cries aloud (verse 2), and finally, through the rest of his song, he progresses to directed, articulate, expectant prayer (verse 3). Don't rush your prayers. Wait and process your emotions in God's presence until the sighs and cries give way to disciplined conversation with Him.

Set aside the morning, the first part of the day, for prayer time. David did, so did Daniel, and so did our greatest model of prayer, Jesus. You may or may not be a morning person. Greg amazes me. No matter how late he was up the night before, no matter what time zone he is in, he will be up early in the morning. Me, not so much! Nevertheless, I still subscribe to the words of the psalmist, who wrote, "O God, You are my God; early will I seek You" (Psalm 63:1). How much better it is when we pray first before we venture out to face the day and its challenges.

Be specific. In Psalm 5 David asks for justice in his situation, and then he asks for personal direction and guidance: "Lead me, O LORD . . . because of my enemies; make Your way straight before my face" (verse 8).

Be hopeful. "I lay my requests before you and wait in expectation" (verse 3, NIV). How confident is a heart that knows and loves God! With each trial and test over the course of his life, David grew in confidence that God not only *could* but *would* deliver him out of his fears.

26: TAKING RESPONSIBILITY

For godly sorrow produces repentance leading to
salvation, not to be regretted; but the sorrow of the
world produces death.

(2 CORINTHIANS 7:10)

I read an interesting tongue-in-cheek quote from Lawrence J.
Peter. He said, "Psychiatry enables us to correct our faults by
confessing our parents' shortcomings."

Of course that doesn't really work very well, does it? As
Christians, it doesn't help us to confess our parents' failures and
sins; we can only confess our own. And that is a difficult thing
to do. It's hard for us to name our sins one by one, to see them
for what they are, to identify them, and not to excuse ourselves.
Because until we are willing to take responsibility for the place
we are in our lives, we will find it very, very difficult to move
forward. If we continue to blame someone or something else, we
will remain stalled in our Christian walk. We can all find plenty
of excuses for our failures: *It's in my genes. It's my parents' fault.
It's that husband of mine. It's all those tough circumstances I faced.
It's my environment. You need to cut me some slack because I've had
it pretty rough.*

But those sorts of excuses never will help us deal with reality.
We need to face up to our own responsibility. Our first parents,
Adam and Eve, set the classic template for blame shifting. We

read after they disobeyed God that "the eyes of both of them were opened, and they knew that they were naked" (Genesis 3:7). Well, what to do now but get on it and stitch up some very itchy and scratchy fig leaf cover-ups to hide behind? And then came the finger pointing. Adam threw Eve under the bus, and she did the same to the serpent.

Greg tells the story of the king of Prussia who was inspecting one of his nation's prisons. He walked through the jail, from cell to cell, talking to the men who had been incarcerated. Each conversation was essentially the same. The prisoner would say, "Help me, your highness. It's not my fault. I was framed! Please get me out of here. I don't deserve this." He finally came to one cell where a man had a different story. He looked the king in the eyes and said, "I am here, my king, because I deserve to be here. I deserve my punishment. I did wrong. I am guilty of a crime, and I only have myself to blame."

The king turned to the guards and said, "Quick! Release this guilty man before he corrupts all of these innocent people!"

We are so unwilling to come out of hiding and into the light. Adam and Eve were afraid of God, so they got busy with their own solution. It was all so temporary! Besides the fact that fig leaves had to be ridiculously uncomfortable, how long would this cover-up hold together? Sadly, it would require the death of an innocent animal for God to make them garments of skin. Before this moment, nothing had ever died. I imagine they watched in horror at the sight of the first drops of blood ever spilled, falling to the ground. All of this prefigured the final sacrifice God would require for our forgiveness. It is only by Christ's suffering and death on the cross that our sins are forgiven.

So let's not run and hide any longer. Instead, let's come running to the only One who can fix and rescue us. Don't forget that He sees everything and knows all about it anyway. Confessing isn't informing God of something He doesn't know.

Until we are willing to acknowledge our sins and short-comings, we will never experience the forgiveness and freedom of Christ that we need so desperately.

Is that enough, then? Is that all it takes, to see our condition and acknowledge it? Is it enough to shake our heads or even shed a few tears over our sin?

No, because Scripture tells us that godly sorrow will produce *repentance* (see 2 Corinthians 7:10). That means we will change our behavior in specific, detectable ways. It's a U-turn and a direction change in our lives.

And nothing less will bring God's blessing.

27: TAKE A STAND

Confess your trespasses to one another, and pray for one another, that you may be healed. The effective, fervent prayer of a righteous man avails much.

(JAMES 5:16)

The night I received Christ, I was with a girlfriend named Cindy. I remember that the speaker challenged those who were making a decision for Jesus to stand up. I did stand up, but it seemed like no one else in that room was standing with me. I leaned over and said to Cindy, "What are you doing just sitting there? Stand up with me!" I remember thinking, *She has to do this.*

So she did. We both prayed the sinner's prayer and received the follow-up materials. In the weeks that followed, however, I realized that it hadn't been Cindy's choice at all. It was my choice *for* her. I had wanted her to make the same decision that I had made, but she hadn't truly made it for herself. In the course of time, it became obvious that she had never received Christ at all; she was just going along with me to please me.

One thing I learned that night is that I need to do what is right and take a stand.

Nehemiah the prophet understood that too. We see him make a very public stand for what is right in Nehemiah 9. One thing about the confession in that chapter . . . it was *very* public. They took it out of the framework of private thought and brought it to the next step. They didn't just rehearse in their minds how distressed and sorry they were for their sins; they published it before everyone and made a public commitment to change.

That is not just an Old Testament concept, by the way.

In the book of James we read, "Therefore confess your sins to each other and pray for each other so that you may be healed. The prayer of a righteous man is powerful and effective" (James 5:16, NIV).

What specifically do you want to see changed in your life, and what do you need to do to get there? Tell the Lord about it, and then tell someone close to you. Confide in a mature, godly friend or your pastor. Let someone else know that you are serious about letting go of a sinful habit and that you want them to pray for you or even hold you accountable to make that change. Until we take steps like these, it will be difficult for us to break free and move forward.

In Nehemiah 9:38 we read, "In view of all this, we are making a binding agreement, putting it in writing, and our leaders, our Levites and our priests are affixing their seals to it" (NIV). The Israelites came up with a plan to show they were serious about a new direction for their lives. They formalized their commitment in writing and then signed it in front of everyone. I'd like to point out three simple things about that written agreement.

It was made by individuals. Each person signed that public document with his or her unique signature. They may have even participated in the sealing of that covenant, each with a unique, individual seal all their own. In the same way, when each of us makes a commitment to Jesus Christ, we make it as an individual. We don't make it with our family or with our friends; we make a personal, individual commitment to walk with Jesus

Christ and to obey Him. We make a commitment to be in His Word and to go to Him daily in prayer. In a sense, it's like standing up and saying, "Yes, Lord, I want to be a part of this. I am doing this, and it's my choice."

It was specific in its requirements, and it was clear in its purpose. These were individual people who participated in that event. It wasn't just a big, faceless crowd. These people put their names on a document and took an oath before God, essentially saying, "This is what we will do. We are serious about this." That was one way they made their decision tangible.

We need to find ways to do that too. We need to find ways to take our spiritual decisions out of the realm of vague, nebulous thoughts or half-hearted effort and show ourselves and others that we are serious, that we mean what we say.

Each signature on the document in Nehemiah 9 was made by an individual. Some of the points in that agreement identified certain sins or specific practices that needed to stop. Other points emphasized practices that needed to be held onto or reinforced.

This is by far the most difficult part about confession and repentance. Some women I've spoken to have such a difficult time identifying specific areas in their lives where they need prayer. Instead, they make vague, general statements that really could apply to anyone. They will pray, "Lord, help me, change me, mold me, make me better." But they hesitate to say, "Lord, I'm letting You know and letting my sisters know that I'm having real trouble with *this . . .*" (naming the struggle or sin).

I can understand the reluctance to speak up in front of others about failures or shortcomings in our lives. But going back to James 5:16, here is something to remember: The more specific we are in our prayers for deliverance from the sins that trouble us and trip us up, the better we are able to receive the forgiveness and healing that could be ours.

28: SIMPLY SPLENDID

Worship the LORD in the splendor of holiness.

(1 CHRONICLES 16:29, ESV)

When slipping into your outfit on Sunday morning, your first priority is to consider the way in which you will prepare yourself to worship God. Of course, this isn't saying that how we dress ourselves for church is the only way to prepare ourselves, but certainly it isn't less than this.

I'm all for "Come just as you are" to Christ. But ladies, really now, once we know and love Him as His own special children, shouldn't we want to represent Him in the best way? (Warning: Let's be careful *not* to use this measuring rod to beat up some new believer who has not had balanced and biblical teaching about modesty.) Let each of us take a minute to think and assess our *own* selves on this often touchy subject.

As I was reading through the Old Testament book of 1 Chronicles, I was fascinated by these words: "the splendor of holiness." When I researched this, I learned that when David was telling the people to proclaim the glory of the Lord before the nations, they were also to worship the Lord in *splendid attire* (see 1 Chronicles 16:29, ESV). I'm not sure the ladies of that time were as concerned about following the trend reports as some of us are. But certainly they must have heard about the request coming from none other than the king himself.

Our bodies are the temple, the sacred dwelling place, of the Holy Spirit of God. While we must consider the beauty and cleanness of our souls as the most important quality, shouldn't we want to reflect, not distract from, the loveliness of His presence that is part of *all* of us? I have often heard women use as an excuse, "God knows my heart." In other words, "I will dress and behave however I may choose."

The fact is, what we *wear* reveals to a watching world something of what we *believe*. Does the way you care for, protect, esteem, use, and, yes, even dress yourself tell of this wonderful truth?

Every part of your being—spirit, soul, and, last but not least, body—will appear in splendor before God. This is what Christianity teaches, and it is what we as Christian women must keep in mind when flipping the pages of the latest *In Style* magazine, trying to decide which look is best for us!

29: THE RIGHT CHOICE

Mary . . . sat at Jesus' feet and heard His word. . . .
[Jesus said,] "Mary has chosen that good part,
which will not be taken away from her."

(LUKE 10:39,42)

The long, slender, oval-shaped window with a magnifying glass icon perches at the top of every webpage I open. At the click of my mouse, in seconds, I can be reading a recipe for mouthwatering *boeuf Bourguignon,* analyzing a sunny outdoor living space, checking out the trendiest pair of platform shoes, or searching for a long-lost childhood friend on Facebook.

I attest to the fact that one need never be bored again. The Internet is an endless source of information and entertainment. However, it is also a place of diversion! How often I sit at my desk, ready to begin work on something, and there the blank window sits open, like my personal magic genie. "Come to me. Your search is my command, Master." *Ha! Master, my foot!*

Am I mastering the machine, or is the machine mastering me?

I walk the aisle in the grocery store, spending twenty minutes looking for the brand of Chex cereal we like because there are too many others crowding the shelves. I want to buy some Chex cereal, but should it be Rice Chex, Corn Chex, Wheat Chex, Multi-Bran Chex, Honey Nut Chex, Chocolate Chex *(my chocoholic granddaughter Lucy would love this!),* Cinnamon Chex, or Apple Cinnamon Chex?

Yikes! No wonder it takes me so long to find what I came in to buy. And just when I figure out the layout of my store (Wheat Chex is on the top right shelf at the end of Aisle 3), they shuffle all the boxes, and I am back to twenty minutes of looking! (And that is when I go in knowing exactly what I want to buy.)

When it comes to choices, we ladies need to have some idea before we go shopping, right? Am I looking for the greatest deal on earth, the tastiest product, or the one packed with the most nutrition per bite . . . hmmm? We need to decide *before* we shop what our criteria should be for making choices.

So many times we go looking on the shelves, distracted by the packaging and clever advertising. Simply put, if you go in with an open mind about shopping, you may end up wasting your time, energy, and money on what doesn't deliver.

I admit that I have found the Internet can be a huge distraction at any time of the day. Five minutes turn into fifteen, and faster than I can type *Amazon.com,* I have wasted another hour! So I had to make some choices and set some boundaries for my growing Internet habit. Before I spend one second skipping around in virtual reality, I spend time *in* reality with my Lord.

Mary of Bethany had choices as well—not as many as we do, but there were choices to make, and she made the right one. There was a gathering of Jesus' disciples at her home. Rooms needed arranging, floors needed sweeping, food needed to be purchased, prepared, and plated. It would fall to the women to do such things, so she and Martha had their work cut out for them.

And yet, above all these good things, which I have no doubt Mary properly accomplished, there was one thing that Mary counted as her greatest priority. I can imagine Martha furiously carving red and white roses out of radishes to garnish the salad bowl. And it began to take its toll on both sisters. While Martha continued to be dragged about by her plans, Mary knew it was time to slip out of her apron and join the disciples to sit at Jesus' feet and listen to His words.

There is always that certain moment when a good thing begins to crowd out the best thing. Can you distinguish when that is, when it's time to *choose* to close your laptop, shut off your smartphone, and instead pick up the Book and hear His voice? Remember, only you can choose that good portion, and with God's help, you can make the right choice!

30: BRINGING THE OLD CATHE BACK

And do not be conformed to this world, but be transformed by the renewing of your mind, that you may prove what is that good and acceptable and perfect will of God.

(ROMANS 12:2)

After I became a Christian, I came to realize that my friendship with Cindy (whom I mentioned in chapter 27) had to change.

Why?

Because day after day as we walked home from school together, Cindy tried her best to pull me back into the old lifestyle, the life I was trying to leave behind to follow the Lord.

At first, excited as I was about my new faith in Jesus, I didn't have much trouble sticking with my commitment. But the longer I stayed with the old crowd, the more difficult it became for me. Cindy, especially, seemed intent on bringing "the old Cathe" back, the one she had been friends with for so many years. That backward tug became oppressive. I felt like I was being worn down. In fact, I did fall away for a while, going back to some of my old ways. But it wasn't fun anymore. I felt miserable about it. There is no one more miserable and unhappy than a Christian who is trying to walk the middle of the road and live two lifestyles simultaneously.

What I needed to do (but didn't completely want to do) was to separate myself from Cindy and that old group of friends.

Maybe there is a "Cindy" in your life as well.

Never doubt it: The world around you will try, as the J. B. Phillips translation of Romans 12:2 so memorably puts it, to "squeeze you into its own mould." Your friends who are not godly, who don't have the mind of Christ, and who don't have the same goals and objectives of walking with the Lord will try to influence you and pull you back into their orbit. Like it or not, the world is not comfortable with a shiny, bright Christian in their midst. To make themselves more comfortable, they'll do their best to dim your light—or put it out altogether.

Day after day that was happening to me. I needed some new friends. I needed to establish new habits. I needed to separate myself from one group and join myself to another—a group of people who loved Jesus and wanted to please Him.

If you are struggling and frequently stumbling in an area of your life, you might need to identify those habits or practices that are making you stumble. If, for instance, you struggle with envy and coveting material things, maybe you shouldn't keep leafing through all of those glossy catalogs, going to certain websites, or watching the shopping network. If you are spending your time looking at magazines filled with ads for cars and houses and clothing you can't afford, you probably need to separate yourself from those. That influence may be wearing you down, causing you to feel discontented, unhappy, or depressed with what God has given you.

It reminds me of the situation the people of Israel faced in Nehemiah 10:

> The rest of the people – priests, Levites, gatekeepers, singers, temple servants and all who separated themselves from the neighboring peoples for the sake of the Law of God, together with their wives and all their sons

and daughters who are able to understand — all these now join their brothers the nobles, and bind themselves with a curse and an oath to follow the Law of God given through Moses the servant of God and to obey carefully all the commands, regulations and decrees of the Lord our Lord. (verses 28-29, NIV)

Three words jump out at me in this passage: *separated, join,* and *together.*

When you think about it, *separated* and *join* are absolute opposites. A dictionary definition of the word *separate* is "to divide or distinguish." In this case, the people identified an area where they were having trouble. They put their finger on it and called it what it was.

In 2 Corinthians 6:14-15, Paul writes, "Don't team up with those who are unbelievers. How can righteousness be a partner with wickedness? How can light live with darkness? What harmony can there be between Christ and the devil? How can a believer be a partner with an unbeliever?" (NLT).

Separate . . . and then *join.* In a second step, you need to form relationships that will encourage you, uplift you, and change your focus. Maybe (as an example) you could spend some time at a Teen Challenge home, a homeless mission, or a nursing home with people who are much worse off than you are. Maybe you should go on a short-term missions trip to another country. Helping others is one sure way to change an unhappy, introspective focus!

If we ask Him for help, the Lord will show us how to deal with those stubborn, struggling areas of our lives in practical ways. But first we have to be honest, identify them, and call them what they are.

The other word that I noted in this passage (in addition to *separated* and *join*) is *together.* "All who separated themselves . . . together with their wives and all their sons and daughters who are able to understand—all these now join their brothers the nobles, and bind themselves with . . . an oath."

I love this. The passage speaks of husbands and wives, sons and daughters. They joined themselves to a group of like-minded people. They partnered with those who would encourage them in their choices and decisions. They helped fortify one another and encourage one another. How we need this! The Christian life was never intended to be lived in isolation. Paul writes, "Therefore encourage one another and build each other up, just as in fact you are doing" (1 Thessalonians 5:11, NIV).

Are your friendships and associations helping you, lifting you, and breathing heart into you, or are they dragging you down like a weight?

Make friends with someone who is spiritually further down the road than you are—someone who will encourage you, challenge you, and inspire you to make positive changes in your life. The Holy Spirit will use the body of Christ to do that in our lives.

When I let go of my relationship with Cindy, God gave me a friend named Jeannie. We had the best time together in high school. Both of us wanted to walk with the Lord, and we lifted each other up through those years. We had prayer times before school together in the morning. We did Bible studies at lunchtime together. We went to Christian camp together. We witnessed for Christ together. Oh yes, we were still two teenage girls with all kinds of struggles and conflicts, but Jeannie and I were walking on the same road together, going in the same direction.

Sadly, Cindy died of a heroin overdose three years after we parted company. The last time I saw her was during a lunch break on our high school campus. As I looked into her dark, half-lidded eyes, she looked so empty, so lost.

"Cindy," I said to her, "why are you doing this to yourself?

Don't you remember the night we both stood to receive Christ? Didn't that mean anything to you? It sure did to me!"

She stared blankly at me and said nothing. And that was our last contact with each other. What a sad story of a wasted life. And if she had persuaded me to leave my Christian faith and follow her back into our old lifestyle, it might have been my story as well.

How thankful I am for the influence of strong Christian friends in my life like Jeannie!

There is a wonderful Scripture in Ecclesiastes 4 that goes like this:

Two are better than one,
    because they have a good return for their work:
If one falls down,
    his friend can help him up.
But pity the man who falls
    and has no one to help him up!
Also, if two lie down together, they will keep warm.
    But how can one keep warm alone?
Though one may be overpowered,
    two can defend themselves.
A cord of three strands is not quickly broken. (verses 9-12, NIV)

Thank God for our brothers and sisters in Christ who sharpen us like "iron sharpens iron" (Proverbs 27:17). Find yourself a sharp Christian friend who will encourage you and spur you on, not just to walk with the Lord but also to serve Him.

Then move forward together . . . and know the incomparable satisfaction of being used by God.

31: SLEEPLESS

You will keep him in perfect peace, whose mind is stayed on You, because he trusts in You.

(ISAIAH 26:3)

woke up early this morning at 2:30 a.m. Soon the list of things I had to do came marching through my mind—like guests arriving too early for a party.

I tried to shoo them out: *Go away until a proper time, when I can do something with you!* And they scampered out, only to linger just outside my conscious thoughts . . . knocking!

When nighttime is interrupted by unwelcome thoughts, concerns, and to-do lists, what can you do? The more you try to push them out, the more aware of them you are!

Here is what I do—and did last night.

First, take them one by one and hand them over to the Lord in prayer. He is able to give grace and wisdom sufficient for each situation. Better yet, forget your needs for a moment and remember all those who are lonely, in pain, suffering, and lost, and pray for God to show them mercy.

Second, reflect on the character of God and all that He has done for you. I focus my sleepless times on praising Him for who He is. I take each letter (A to Z) and name the great riches I have been given in Christ. (A, accepted in the Beloved; B, blessed with every spiritual blessing; C, chosen in Him before the foundations of the world . . .)

Third, meditate on the great "I am" statements of Christ:

- "I am . . . the Bread of Life."
- "I am . . . the Light of the World."
- "I am . . . the Door."
- "I am . . . the Good Shepherd."
- "I am . . . the Resurrection and the Life."
- "I am . . . the Way, the Truth, and the Life."
- "I am . . . the True Vine."

How wonderful these statements are! Many times, I can fall sweetly asleep with thoughts that comfort and edify. At other times, like last night, I went through all my lists and still didn't get back to sleep for hours.

But so what?

At the very least, it was time not wasted!

32: LAUGH . . . BE HAPPY!

Blessed is the man . . .

(PSALM 1:1)

Christians are happy people. If we're not, we *ought* to be. Some people imagine that believers don't know how to have fun or that we lack a fully developed sense of humor. All I can say is, spend five minutes with my husband, and you will realize that Christians certainly do know how to laugh and have fun.

The first word of the first psalm begins with the word *blessed*. The word in Hebrew means exactly what you would think it would mean: "happy."

David and the other psalmists loved to use this word:

Blessed is he whose transgression is forgiven, whose sin is covered. (32:1)

Blessed is the nation whose God is the LORD. (33:12)

Blessed is that man who makes the LORD his trust. (40:4)

Blessed are those who dwell in Your house;
They will still be praising You.
Blessed is the man whose strength is in You. (84:4-5)

And on and on it goes. The Psalms overflow with blessing—even when it rises out of dark, difficult circumstances and pain.

It's the same for us.

The whole concept of the Psalms and singing to the Lord underlies our Christian heritage. Did you know the music and singing of the Christian church is unusual among the world's religions? So many religions of the world have nothing to compare with the great body of hymns and songs and choruses that we as believers possess and enjoy.

Christians have a great anthology of hymns and songs that go back to the very earliest days because the church of Jesus Christ, worshiping as we do a risen King, is a happy church, a singing church. Let's face it: God's Word on happiness is better than anyone else's, anywhere.

When Jonathan Edwards was just eighteen, he preached his first sermon. (Unfortunately, most would only think of Edwards as that angry preacher who wrote the tract "Sinners in the Hands of an Angry God.") His first sermon, however, was titled "Christian Happiness." It had three outstanding points:

1. Our bad things will turn out for good.
2. Our good things can never be taken away from us.
3. The best things are yet to come.

So it's appropriate that the very first line of the very first psalm would begin, "[Happy] is the man . . ."

33: A BEAUTIFUL LIFE

And let the beauty of the LORD our God be upon us.
(PSALM 90:17)

What makes something beautiful?

Whether it is music, painting, gardening, cooking, or fashion, there is a quality that captivates us, but which is sometimes hard to quantify or define. We want to stop and look, listen and touch. Beauty draws us in. We want to linger, take it in.

As believers, we want this quality about our lives. In an intriguing passage in Titus 2:10, we are told we must live our lives in such a way that we may "adorn" the gospel of Christ. But how can we make something already so beautiful . . . *more beautiful?* We can't. I'm sure the gospel doesn't need embellishing, nor can we in any way add to its perfection.

So what could this possibly mean? The thought behind our adorning the gospel is that our conduct (manner of living) puts it on attractive display. Pause for a moment and consider that we have the responsibility and privilege of influencing how people think about Christianity. Those around us who don't believe are observing how we live, the words we speak, the way we dress, and the things we love. We are the representatives of what a Christian life should look like. Whether it is changing a diaper, studying for a test, or forgiving a wrong done, we can make the teachings about our God and Savior attractive.

It is a sobering thought that we have the power to commend —or discredit—what we profess. Only Christ lived a perfectly beautiful life. But as we spend time in His presence, learning from Him and being transformed by His grace, we can hope to display this kind of beautiful life and draw others to Christ.

Precious Lord, I want to spend time in Your presence that I might be beautifully adorned with the truth and power of Your Word. I want others to be drawn to You because of the beauty of the gospel I seek to display in my words and actions. Amen.

34: FIFTY SHADES OF GREY?

Blessed is the man who walks not in the counsel of
the ungodly, nor stands in the path of sinners, nor
sits in the seat of the scornful.

(Psalm 1:1)

As of this writing, the fastest-selling paperback in America is
Fifty Shades of Grey.

That is certainly a book title for our times. The world
we live in loves to portray everything in shades of grey.

Twenty-first-century people don't like to make moral judgments of any kind (unless it's against conservative Christians)
and prefer to view the world as a blur of good, bad, and indiffer-
ent. "Well," you will hear people say, "that might be wrong for
me, but it may not be wrong for *her*."

Psalm 1 is known as a wisdom psalm. It begins by describing
what a righteous person is *not* like. Isn't that interesting? It
doesn't begin with a description of what the righteous person
looks like and does, but with what such a man or woman does
not do. You might say they are described negatively. They *don't*
walk in the counsel of the ungodly, they *don't* stand in the path
of sinners, and they *don't* sit in the seat of mockers.

Verse 2, then, tells us what they *are* like: They are like a tree
planted by the rivers of water. Wisdom literature loves to present

life as an either-or choice. It is very black and very white, and there is no mixing.

Our culture doesn't like things portrayed in black-and-white anymore. In the old movies, it used to be easy to pick out the good guys from the bad guys. Not anymore. As a matter of fact, it's far more common for the plot to take a twist—leaving the guy with the white hat as the real villain.

Most people think of their progress in life like rungs on some great cosmic ladder. At the very top of the ladder, you have someone like Mother Teresa or St. Francis of Assisi or Billy Graham. And at the bottom of the ladder are Adolf Hitler and Osama bin Laden and all the treacherous men and women of history. And the rest of us? Well, we're somewhere in the middle, trying to make our climb—and hopefully we're closer to the top than the bottom.

But that is not how Psalm 1 portrays us. Rather than the rungs and the horizontal lines of a ladder, we have one very straight line that divides us right down the middle into two groups: It says you are either godly or ungodly.

On one side of that line, we are told that a godly person does *not* walk in the counsel of the ungodly.

The word *counsel* here refers to the realm of the mind—how we think about things. What does it mean for us in the twenty-first century to refuse to walk in the counsel of ungodly people? Does it speak to the music we listen to? The websites we frequent? The TV shows we watch? The books we read? The movies we attend? The magazines we page through?

Sure, it speaks to all of those things because they engage our eyes and ears and influence our minds.

The world shouts at us every moment of the day. Its messaging never stops. Psalm 1 warns us to protect our thoughts and to be careful about what we expose ourselves to.

DON'T STAND SO CLOSE

Most of us can imagine the scene: Robin Hood and Little John happen to meet on a long, narrow bridge, each carrying a stout staff in his hands. Since neither one will give way or give in, blows and insults are traded back and forth—until one gets knocked off the bridge and into the creek below. Nowadays when we use the words "don't stand in my way," we're thinking about someone blocking our way.

Is this what Psalm 1 means by "stands in the path of sinners"? Actually, no. This is one of those Hebrew euphemisms or figures of speech that gets lost in translation. What this expression really means is that the godly don't stand *in the way that ungodly people stand.*

When you hear the word *sinner* or *ungodly*, you might find yourself exclusively thinking about evil people doing horrible, despicable things. But just for a moment, I'd like you to delete that image from your mind.

When you read the word *ungodly*, do you picture that nice neighbor of yours who walks her dog in the park every day, says hello to you, and makes polite conversation?

Probably not.

After all, this is the lady who asks about your kids, comments on the weather, and seems so pleasant, kind, and sweet. But when you make any effort to bring up the subjects of faith, God, and eternal things, she gets very quiet and uncomfortable and shows zero interest. She may discuss them for a moment, but only in the most general, vague, fuzzy, noncommittal sort of way. It becomes clear that she lives for the here and now and hasn't given much (if any) thought to the meaning and purpose of life. She lives with this world in view and not much else. Period. In other words, she is ungodly, which technically means "without God." She is an ungodly woman, personable and pleasant though she may be.

So what does it mean to stand in the path of the ungodly? It means that you begin to think like she does. You begin to define life in terms of the here and now. You give priority to the pleasures of the moment over the long-term goals of living a life that pleases and honors God.

When you refuse to stand in her way, it means you have chosen to live life with eternity in view and make choices and sacrifices that may not be easy or very pleasing in the moment but that have long-term implications for a life well-lived.

You are choosing to have an eternal perspective.

But what happens if you begin to be influenced by an ungodly view? What happens if you find yourself thinking of this life only and make choices based on the desires and whims of the moment? It won't be very long before you find yourself sitting in the seat of the scornful.

WHERE ARE YOU HEADING?

Consider the following conversation from John Bunyan's *Pilgrim's Progress:*

> Obstinate: What are the things you seek, since you leave all the world to find them?

> Christian: I seek an *Inheritance incorruptible, undefiled, and that fadeth not away* [1 Peter 1:4], and it is laid up in Heaven, and safe there, to be bestowed, at the time appointed, on them that diligently seek it [Hebrews 11:16]. Read it so, if you will, in my Book.

> Obstinate: Away with your Book; will you go back with us, or no?[1]

I'm reminded again of my sophomore year in high school, not long after I came to Christ. For a while, unsure of what else to do, I began to reconnect with my old non-Christian friends. Slowly, imperceptibly at first, I began to see the world through their eyes again. I began to buy into their values and participate in their activities, and it wasn't long before I was joining them in looking down my nose at those narrow-minded, lame Christians who were always quoting Scripture.

I began to *scorn* them.

Thank God, it wasn't the end of my story. Graciously, He opened my eyes and brought me back. I left those old associations, found some new Christian friends, and resumed my walk with Jesus Christ. But it was a lesson to me on how quickly a believer can lose his or her grip on all those precious, eternal truths we hold dear. We need to be very careful, no matter who we are, no matter how long we have been in the faith.

Make no mistake: *Sitting with the scornful* is a tragic place to land. If you stand long enough in the counsel of the ungodly and walk long enough in the path of those who live for this life only, you will find yourself becoming affected by their apathetic or cynical attitudes toward truths you once held dear. Not only that, but you won't be able to process the trials, challenges, and opportunities that come into your life in the right way. You will misunderstand God's working in your life and become hardened by the things that happen to you.

It is easy, very easy, to settle into the seat of the scornful. To sit in this place means to finally settle into the views of those who despise and ridicule Christian beliefs and put down those who hold to biblical values.

You might say to yourself, "Well, I would never end up in a place like that." But don't kid yourself. Any of us are capable of slipping into this mindset when we neglect the Bible, prayer, and fellowship with other believers. Any of us, if we're not on guard, can be swayed by the dominant, godless viewpoints of our culture.

Back to the question Obstinate posed to Christian: "Will you go back with us, or no?"

I have a three-word warning from Jesus: "Remember Lot's wife."

For better or worse, the stand you take today will color the decisions you make tomorrow.

35: A COMMON FAITH

Therefore, brethren, stand fast and hold the
traditions which you were taught, whether by word
or our epistle.

(2 Thessalonians 2:15)

We had a family reunion this past spring in the green hills overlooking Glendora. It was a picture-perfect Southern California evening, with amber sunlight warming our faces under a trellis in the backyard. Aunt Willie had draped the trellis with pale yellow fabric and hung white paper lanterns that looked like gigantic moons swinging over our heads. Everything was cast in a warm glow. Delightful fragrances, drifting from the nearby kitchen, beckoned us to the feast.

All the aunts had prepared a traditional southern meal, calling to mind the many we had enjoyed together when Mama Stella, Greg's grandmother, was still with us. I'll never forget the trips Greg and I would make out to Yucaipa to visit her and Daddy Charles. She'd always be apologizing that she hadn't fixed "anything special." But from the moment we walked in the door, we would be greeted by the scent of wonderful, home-prepared food drifting from the kitchen. We were like the dog in the old cartoons who floated in the air, hugging himself every time he got a treat. I'd be salivating, looking at her "not-so-special" meal of pork chops, collard greens, fried green tomatoes, milk gravy, and, of course, her *pièces de résistance*: those heavenly buttermilk biscuits. The table was loaded with so many of her homemade preserved jams, jellies, pickles, and relishes that it would rival any shelf at Dean & DeLuca.

Every time we've gathered since our beloved Christopher, Mama Stella, and Daddy Charles went to heaven, I picture them eating and feasting at the table with our King. Maybe Mama Stella and Martha of Bethany, wearing aprons, are stirring the gravy and baking biscuits for a feast beyond our imagination. However, back in Glendora that night, we did our best to celebrate with fried chicken, mashed potatoes and gravy, black-eyed peas, green beans, and, of course, the biscuits and cornbread. Our plates weren't nearly big enough!

The real feast, however, involved something more than food. It also included the celebration of our common faith. This is a faith that has sprung from the McDaniel's and Fowler's sturdy country roots in Friendship, Arkansas, and has held this family together over the years.

Even though the life of Greg's mother, Charlene, was characterized by turbulent years of wandering and rebellion, the ties to her godly family helped secure a place for Greg and gave him at least a measure of security. Despite the tumult of Greg's growing-up years, Mama Stella managed to plant seeds of faith deep in his heart and memory. In fact, the seeds of faith that she faithfully planted through the years sprang up all over the place. Aunt Willie and Uncle Fred, who established a mission to the unfortunate of Skid Row, had also been impacted by Mama Stella's life and lived out a strong, resilient faith that a young Greg couldn't miss.

This great family circle, now bigger with the lives of little ones, will hold fast together here on earth, and soon, we'll join those who are waiting for us in heaven. As wonderful as a reunion in Glendora might be, heaven will offer a better family gathering and a better feast than we could begin to imagine here on earth.

So we're saving our best appetites for heaven, looking forward to the dessert table that will overflow with even more than the one that was before us that night. It will be better than Elsie's berry cobbler, Aunt Flo's chocolate cake, or even Aunt Willie's croissant bread pudding. It's hard for the little ones to imagine anything better than chocolate sauce on creamy, hand-churned vanilla ice cream—but it isn't for those of us who are longing and hungering for that part of us that is out of sight, but never out of our hearts.

In the meantime, we celebrate the tie that binds and tell stories of the old days . . . and have maybe just one more bite of that bread pudding.

36: WHAT IT MEANS TO MEDITATE

In His law he meditates day and night.

(Psalm 1:2)

meditate: to chew over, cogitate, consider, contemplate, deliberate, entertain, eye, kick around, ponder, mull (over), perpend, pore (over), question, resolve, ruminate, study, think (about or over), turn, weigh, wrestle (with).

Meditation is more than just learning.

If you were to take a yoga class, the instructors would no doubt encourage you to "empty your mind" of all conscious thought. In other words, set aside your worries, your concerns, and the thoughts that come to your mind, trying to achieve a big mental blank.

That is what is known as Eastern meditation, and it supposedly brings you to a place of great relaxation. But what then? *Who knows what will seek to fill that emptiness?* Remember the warning in Ephesians 6: "Our fight is not against any physical enemy: it is against organisations and powers that are spiritual. We are up against the unseen power that controls this dark world, and spiritual agents from the very headquarters of evil" (verse 12, ph). The fact is, we don't want to be emptying our minds, but filling them with the powerful Word of God.

Christian meditation is nothing at all like Eastern meditation; it's exactly the opposite. Christian mediation is almost like hyper thinking, where you take words and concepts and drill them down deep into your conscious mind. Another word for it is *pondering*. It is going over the truths of Scripture to the point where they capture your heart and move your emotions.

Christian meditation takes time. You don't open your Bible and immediately find yourself moved by emotion. Or at least it doesn't work that way for me. I need to give myself enough time in God's Word so that it's not just an academic exercise. I try to get to a point where I am hearing God's Holy Spirit speaking to me.

Sometimes when I hear God speak to me through His Word, it brings tears. Sometimes it brings me great peace. At other times, I find myself incredibly blessed, and joy begins to bubble up within me.

Not that it's always that way. But that is the goal I aim for: a heart response to what I encounter in the pages of God's Word. Christian meditation is more than just thinking; it is being moved by what you are thinking.

The Hebrew word for *meditate* speaks of muttering and murmuring, talking to yourself under your breath. Does that ever happen to you? Do you ever mumble to yourself as you walk around the house? I think the older you get, the more you do this!

Have you ever had someone write you an e-mail or say something to you that offended or hurt you deeply? Maybe it was something that was said about you or something you heard someone say about you. Chances are, you took that information and went over every single word of it. Every word was packed with meaning, and you tried to imagine this person's motivation for doing or saying something that wounded you. It affects you, doesn't it? It stirs up your emotion.

In a more positive way, think of a love letter—maybe the

first love letter you ever received from your husband or boyfriend. (Do people still write love letters anymore, or do we just text them?) You go over each word, trying to extract the maximum amount of meaning. In fact, you are *meditating* on those words.

That's what we are to do with God's Word. We turn it over in our minds. We ask questions. We think about its implications. We personalize it. Perhaps we even memorize it. And then, in a moment when you weren't even consciously thinking about that Bible passage, it suddenly begins speaking to you, and you hear God's voice. Maybe it's in the middle of the night or just before dawn. You're only half awake, but the words of some Scripture start speaking into your mind, steering you toward biblical thought.

Not all of us do this perfectly. We are all beginners, and we are all learning in this process. But as we do, we are learning what it means to be "blessed."

37: RUNNING UP A DOWN ESCALATOR

"Abide in Me, and I in you. As the branch cannot
bear fruit of itself, unless it abides in the vine,
neither can you, unless you abide in Me."

(JOHN 15:4)

I just finished my morning run. *Whew* . . . it sure is amazing
how quickly one can lose the "edge" on fitness. A couple weeks
off, and I feel it!

Life can sometimes feel like trying to run up a down escala-
tor. This is true of all disciplines, from playing tennis to playing
the piano to learning French. If we don't practice, we won't hold
on to, much less improve, our skills.

What a blessing to know that the principle of abiding in
Jesus Christ, the Vine, and in God's Word will bear the spiritual
fruit we desire. It won't be our constant, breathless efforts that
determine our fruitfulness, but our remaining connected to His
life-giving power.

38: TREES AND CHAFF

He is like a tree planted by streams of water, which yields its fruit in season and whose leaf does not wither. Whatever he does prospers.

(PSALM 1:3, NIV)

In some parts of our world, this metaphor is a little more difficult to understand. In Hawaii, or Southeast Asia where I grew up, there are two seasons: *wet* and *wetter*. If you drop a few seeds into the soil, in a few years there will be a jungle.

But the climate in Israel, where the Bible was written, is very similar to the climate of where we live now in Southern California. The rains come in late winter and early spring, turning the hills green and filling the dry riverbeds with water. And there is life. Then comes summer, fall, and the dry Santa Ana winds. Everything dries up and is parched and crackling. All that spring green is just a memory. It has turned into dry brush that will leap into flame if it's touched by a spark.

God's Word says that the righteous person will not wither up and die, even in the face of harsh challenges and adverse situations. The righteous person has roots that go beyond the circumstances in which they are living. These roots tap into the nature, character, strength, and power of God Himself. The believer's roots tap into life-giving moisture beneath the surface of the hard ground, where people can't see. But what people *do* see are the results of that invisible nourishment and refreshment in a believer's life, and it makes them curious.

How does she stay so fresh, so peaceful, with all that's going on in her life? How does she keep going with so many bad things happening to her? How does she do it?

The person who delights in God's Word is putting down those roots, and it will be one of the most important things you ever do. Those are the roots that will stabilize you, nourish you, and keep your spirit fresh, even when you find yourself in difficult or heartbreaking life circumstances.

Your leaf will not wither.

You will be fruitful in season.

You will draw your ultimate hope and meaning from God Himself, not from events or situations or circumstances.

As Psalm 73:26 says, "My flesh and my heart may fail, but God is the strength of my heart and my portion forever" (NIV). Believe me when I say that if you live long enough, sooner or later you will find yourself in a circumstance with news where your flesh and heart will fail you.

"But God is the strength of my heart."

In spite of hardships and tragedies and deep disappointments in life, you will find a stream flowing underneath the surface that will be the strength of your life.

BLOWN BY THE WIND

> Not so the wicked!
>> They are like chaff
>> that the wind blows away. (Psalm 1:4, NIV)

Chaff is also botanical in nature, an illustration drawn from the natural world just like the tree. Sometimes I think we picture the godly person as being like a beautiful, flourishing tree in contrast to the ungodly, who are like dried-up desert bushes or maybe weeds that grow on a path and become trampled. But the comparison is even more stark than that. The illustration is not between a healthy tree and a dried-up bush or clump of weeds. No, the illustration is between something that is alive and something that is *dead*.

Chaff has no life in it.

Chaff never will grow or change.

Chaff is worthless.

When I was a little girl, we lived in the Philippines, Thailand, and Malaysia. In each of these countries I loved to watch the local girls heaping up rice on big, woven trays. Then they would toss the rice into the air, allowing the wind to separate the hulls and blow them away. It always amazed me to see how they would never miss or drop a single grain. The chaff, however, would simply fly away, blown by the slightest breeze — and not even the wild chickens scratching around wanted anything to do with it.

The Scriptures are painting for us a stark picture of the ungodly. They are weightless. They are lifeless. And they are perishing. That is how God views them. Those who choose to live their lives apart from God with only a horizontal view of life "will not stand in the judgment" nor "in the assembly of the righteous" (verse 5, NIV). From God's perspective, they have no weight and no value.

It makes me think of King Belshazzar in Babylon, who read God's handwriting on the wall: "You have been weighed in the balances, and found wanting" (Daniel 5:27).

When you and I step on the bathroom scale in the morning, most of us wish we weighed less. But when we step on God's heavenly scale, we want that needle to go up rather than down. We want our lives to be heavy. We want lives that count for something.

C. S. Lewis wrote a fictional book called *The Great Divorce* that described how residents of hell could choose to take a bus holiday and visit the outskirts of heaven. As the bus drew nearer and nearer to that bright celestial land, however, the people on the bus became less and less "solid." In fact, you could see right through them. They were ethereal, like ghosts. When they left the bus and tried to walk on the heavenly lawn, the blades of grass would almost pierce right through their feet. If a leaf from a heavenly tree fell on them, it would crush them. Their lives had no substance. They had no weight at all.

It is a graphic illustration of how God views the ungodly: *"They are like chaff that the wind blows away."* The path of the righteous, however, "is like the first gleam of dawn, shining ever brighter till the full light of day" (Proverbs 4:18, NIV).

39: AND THEN WHAT?

The days of our lives are seventy years; and if by
reason of strength they are eighty years, yet their
boast is only labor and sorrow; for it is soon cut
off, and we fly away.

(PSALM 90:10)

One delightful aspect about bike riding with a large group is
that every ten minutes or so, you find yourself riding next to
someone different.

It was an *Endless Summer* kind of day—we could feel the
cool breeze blowing off the Pacific, the sun shining warm on our
arms and noses as we pedaled south on Pacific Coast Highway
through Seal Beach, Huntington Beach, and on to Corona Del
Mar. This perfect day was about as good as it gets on earth.

Conversations on bicycles aren't usually significant. Most
have to do with how many miles you've clocked that week or
what preferred concoction you have in your water bottle. But a
conversation with one man started something like this.

"Next year," he said, "I'll have made enough money to retire.
And then, I will get in even better shape, ride my bike all day,
every day, take it easy, and go on long vacations!"

Such were the daydreams of one forty-year-old cyclist: cruis-
ing up to the sunset years.

I listened, contemplated for a moment the sober reality of

my future and my children's future . . . and felt a twinge of envy. He and his wife were youngish (forty is young to me now), newly married, with one adorable, very privileged daughter.

Their voices rose and fell as they talked on — so very pleasant, like a sailboat headed off to Catalina. The miles ticked on my odometer. They talked, and I tried to imagine what it would be like to have a sense of such financial security . . . all blue skies, endless stretches of palm tree–lined roads, pleasant conversations on bicycles, and postcard sunsets.

At times like these the Holy Spirit will gently nudge or shake you back to truth: *Get a grip, girl. Is that the extent of a life well-lived? Then what? What about ten billion years into eternity? Will a fat 401K provide what you need that far into the future?*

At this point, I couldn't help myself. I am a pastor's wife, and sermonizing is, well, irresistible at times.

"Wow, I guess you've been thinking about your future. Hey, this reminds me of a story that Jesus once told."

I couldn't see whether he rolled his eyes behind his mirror-lensed Oakleys or not, so I continued.

"Jesus said there was this guy who'd made quite a fortune for himself. So much so that he planned to build even bigger warehouses so he could expand his business, kick back, and take life easy. Only, headed around the corner, there was one problem he hadn't counted on. You see, that night God said to him, 'Tonight is your last night, and now who will get the earthly wealth you have acquired?'

"And the guy dies without ever realizing his dreams on earth and — worse yet — he had nothing to show for his life, in eternity.

"Then Jesus said, 'So it is with anyone who may be rich in this life but isn't rich in God's eyes.'"

There was an uncomfortable pause, and then, a moment later, the light changed. The group picked the pace back up; the conversation was over. It can be like that. As John Lennon sang, "Life is what happens to you when you're busy making other plans." Unfortunately for this guy, just a year later the economy went in the tank—along with his plans for early retirement.

Proverbs 23:5 says, "Cast but a glance at riches, and they are gone, for they will surely sprout wings and fly off to the sky like an eagle" (NIV). No, I have nothing against saving for the future. It's a wise thing to do. But it's foolish to think *only* about the here and now.

I have had an image in my mind lately, a picture that reminds me of how quickly time passes. It's a handful of pearls being dropped casually, rhythmically, one by one by one, from our fingertips. These pearls (each of us is given an undisclosed number) are slipping by every day—precious, irreplaceable. So before the next pearl slips through your fingers, ask yourself this question: *If this were my last day on earth, what matters most?* Would you need to make some drastic shifts in your value system?

Remember to assess your values in the light of heaven's economy. Are you rich toward God? What does He prize most? Whatever it is that the Spirit of God may reveal to you, I hope and pray that you won't waste another precious pearl.

40: SHORT, SIMPLE SURRENDER

Continue to work out your salvation with fear and trembling, for it is God who works in you to will and to act according to his good purpose.

(PHILIPPIANS 2:12-13, NIV)

One of my favorite movies is *Luther,* starring Joseph Fiennes. In it we see a young Martin Luther who is continually tormented by his sins and failure. Time after time he confesses his sins, but each time he tries harder to be good, he fails. Then comes a pivotal scene, my favorite in the whole movie, where his confessor admonishes him.

The priest says, "Martin, look to Christ, bind yourself to Christ. Say to Him, 'I am Yours. Save me.'" And the priest repeats the words again, slowly. "I . . . am . . . Yours . . . save . . . me."

In the next scene you see Luther prostrated on the cathedral floor, face on the ground, arms spread out, whispering, "I am Yours. Save me."

That is a short, simple surrender.

But isn't that a paradox?

How could surrender be short and, of all things, *simple*? Aren't surrender and freedom at odds with each other? Doesn't surrendering mean you are coming under some list of laws, restrictions, or rules? Where is the freedom here? How does that portray liberty in any sense of the word?

Let's look a little more closely into a handful of verses from Psalm 119:

> I have kept my feet from every evil path
> so that I might obey your word. (verse 101, NIV)

The psalmist is saying that he held back, refrained his feet, and refused every evil path.

> I have not departed from your laws,
> for you yourself have taught me. (verse 102, NIV)

When the psalmist says, "I have not departed," it means that he has not looked away from God's Word and the vital truths he learned from God Himself.

> I have taken an oath and confirmed it,
> that I will follow your righteous laws. (verse 106, NIV)

In the New King James Version, verse 106 says, "I will keep Your righteous judgments." He will keep his oath to God just as someone would be a keeper of a door or a keeper of some incredibly valuable treasure. He will guard and protect it.

> The wicked have set a snare for me,
> but I have not strayed from your precepts. (verse 110, NIV)

The psalmist maintains that he has not become careless, straying off the path and stumbling into the pits and snares.

> My heart is set on keeping your decrees
> to the very end. (verse 112, NIV)

Again, the New King James Version says, "I have inclined my heart to perform Your statutes." The word *inclined* means that I have bent down, I have stretched out, I have held His Word high in my heart to make sure I perform it. My heart is set!

These verses speak of real effort, don't they? The psalmist is diligent about these things. You don't see anything of a sleepy, lackadaisical attitude that just shrugs its shoulders and says, "*Que sera, sera,* whatever will be, will be." I'm reminded of the apostle Paul's words, when he wrote, "Continue to work out your salvation with fear and trembling, for it is God who works in you to will and to act according to his good purpose" (Philippians 2:12-13, NIV).

The psalmist shows great effort in his desire to live for the Lord. He says, in effect, "Lord, I have Your standards here, and now I am going to apply myself to these standards with all my heart."

We all want to be changed as Christians. I don't want to be as selfish tomorrow as I am today. I don't want to be as prideful and self-absorbed tomorrow as I am today. I don't want to be as petty and unforgiving tomorrow as I am today. I want to change. I want to grow in the grace and knowledge of my Lord and Savior, Jesus Christ. We all want to improve and be conformed into His image.

But how do we accomplish that? We do it through several disciplines. One of them is the discipline of obedience.

To be honest, there is something in me—something in all of us, I imagine—that doesn't really like that word *obedience*. It's a word with hard edges and (at least initially) is not very appealing. We would rather focus on all that God has done for us rather than on how we should be responding to His great gift of salvation.

Why does obedience and the thought of coming under authority sound so unappealing to us today? Even the biblical words *master* and *bondslave* make some of us bristle.

The words may be particularly difficult for Americans. After all, freedom is in our national DNA. As a nation we look back on that time when we threw off the yoke of colonial rule, rejecting the authority of the British king. Our ancestors pursued a nation where they might live and worship as they pleased. One of our earliest national mottos was "Don't tread on me."

Sometimes we Americans think that liberty means freedom from restrictions or freedom from rules that might keep us from fulfilling our heart's desire.

In fact, that is the way most modern people think. But it hasn't always been that way. In previous eras, most people would have accepted the fact that we are not completely free. We have obligations. We are obligated to obey our parents. We are obligated to our spouses to stay married. We are obligated to take care of and raise our children at great cost and sacrifice to our own personal happiness.

But nowadays most people say, "No one is going to tell me what to do. How dare you tell me what I need? I will decide that for myself!"

What we all need is to let go of that *I-can-do-it-myself* attitude. Coming under God's authority is a prescription for peace and contentment. I know this isn't easy, and I know that—at first glance—it seems like a paradox.

May it start today for you and me.

Short, simple surrender.

41: ARE YOU PRAYING FOR SOMEONE?

He saw that there was no man, and wondered that
there was no intercessor.

(ISAIAH 59:16)

The Spirit Himself makes intercession for us.

(ROMANS 8:26)

"I will pour . . . the Spirit of grace and
supplication."

(ZECHARIAH 12:10)

In the early seventies, my oldest sister was in her first year of
college. I was an idealistic fourteen-year-old, enamored by the
romantic notions of the hippie movement.

One night, I tagged along with my two sisters to what we
thought was a concert in the student lounge. Before the music
began, we sat on the lawn of the campus, getting high. Three
people walked over to our little huddle and began to talk to us
about God. Something strange and unfamiliar stirred in my
heart for the first time.

We wandered into the lounge, listened to some rock band
play, and heard a testimony followed by a simple gospel message.
I alone stood up to pray, heart pounding, so self-conscious
among the seated college crowd.

That was the night I gave my life to Christ. Some forty-plus years later, I'm writing this in gratitude to that someone who prayed for my salvation.

Someone had a burden for students.

Someone booked the lounge that night.

Someone invited a preacher and musicians to whom I could relate.

Someone put up posters and invited kids like me to come.

Someone cared about four girls sitting on the college lawn, getting high.

Someone spoke simply and clearly enough for a fourteen-year-old to get it!

Someone sat with me after the concert to follow up after I prayed the sinner's prayer.

I was given a small gospel of John that someone else had paid for.

And three days later, someone wrote a letter and made a phone call, inviting me to go to church that week.

My life was changed . . . forever.

Every facet of that evening was an important link in the chain of events that transformed my life and, later on, the lives of my sisters, my brother, and our family.

This is the first time in more than forty years that I have wondered, *Who was it that prayed for me?* Someone. Now I feel the Holy Spirit asking me, *Whom are you praying for?*

Precious Savior, I thank You that You are my personal Savior and Lord. Help me to be faithful to pray for my unsaved family, friends, and neighbors. Help me to find ways to engage them so they might hear and respond to Your invitation of salvation. Amen.

42: BEAUTY MATTERS

And we all, with unveiled face, beholding the glory
of the Lord, are being transformed into the same
image from one degree of glory to another. For this
comes from the Lord who is the Spirit.

(2 CORINTHIANS 3:18, ESV)

got a call today from a friend with a skin-care business that has
an anti-aging line of products. (Now why do you suppose she
might be calling *me*?)

So I got to thinking, what makes a woman beautiful? Poor
Eleanor Rigby, who "waits at the window, wearing the face that
she keeps in a jar by the door." She's never figured it out. Make
no mistake, external beauty matters—what we wear, the style of
our hair, the shade of lipstick—because God created nature
beautiful as well as functional.

But it's the adorning of our hearts that should first occupy
our thoughts. Five minutes at the cosmetics counter won't fix
this. A true makeover happens only as we behold our Savior and
His loveliness. And this takes a lifetime!

43: IDOL FACTORIES

Turn away my eyes from looking at worthless
things, and revive me in Your way.

(PSALM 119:37)

My little three-year-old granddaughter Lucy loves candy.
This child is definitely her father's daughter because
Christopher was the same way. He and she could sniff out
candy when there was no candy. The other day I walked into my
breakfast nook, and there was Lucy, *climbing the bookshelves* to
reach a little gold mesh bag with a few chocolate coins inside. I
had placed them on that high bookshelf to remove a source of
temptation — from her and me! I knew she wouldn't see them up
there because *I* could barely see them up there. But somehow
Lucy had either sniffed out that little chocolate stash or her eyes
had caught a glint of the gold mesh. She had fixated on that
chocolate and was determined to claim it.

But it isn't just children, is it? We adults get fixated too.
(Including yours truly.)

Everyone is under the control of something. As Bob Dylan
used to sing, you "gotta serve somebody."

There are so many things in this world that compete for
control in your heart, mind, and life. The simple (if unflatter-
ing) fact is this: You can't resist these things in your own strength
and by your own determination.

In Psalm 119:37, the psalmist cries out to God in prayer saying, "Turn away my eyes from looking at worthless things, and revive me in Your way." Notice what he is saying here: "Lord, I know that my eyes are fixed on worthless things. My time and attention are absorbed by things that ultimately have no value. As much as I want to turn away from these things, I find that they control me! I need Your help, Lord, because I can't stop myself. I am *fixed* on these things, and I need You to break me free."

The word *worthless* in this verse is a Hebrew euphemism for the word *idol.* The writer is saying, "Turn my eyes away from looking at anything that has become the idol of my life."

Every one of us worships something or someone. It could be a relationship. It could be your own appearance. It could be your career. It could be the opinion of other people and what they think of you. We all have things that fight for control of our hearts and lives. And how much worse the battle becomes when we are not living under the control of and with the help of the Holy Spirit.

Jonah 2:8 uses the same word for *worthless* when the prophet says (from deep under the ocean, covered with muck in the digestive tract of a great fish), "Those who cling to worthless idols forfeit the grace that could be theirs" (NIV). For Jonah the worthless idol may have been his national pride. Why else was he so resistant to go and preach to the Ninevites if not for the fact they were the enemies of his people? Any time we do not worship God above all else, we begin to drift toward idols.

We don't want to fix our eyes on worthless things. Life is way too short to waste time and energy being focused on empty pursuits. Nevertheless, through the course of our lives, you and I will continue to be drawn toward them. Let's face it: Inevitably our eyes will stray in that direction. As Timothy Keller wrote in his insightful book *Counterfeit Gods,* "An idol has such a controlling position in your heart that you can spend most of your passion and energy, your emotional and financial resources, on it without a second thought."[1]

Last week Greg was reading an ad in the newspaper about a top Italian dress designer who was designing clothing for a local chain of clothing stores. Greg said, "Hey, this designer Marni is showing a line of her clothing at H&M. You ought to check it out."

Great idea, Greg! So I called up H&M and found out that the mall store was featuring her stuff and would be opening their doors early at 8:00 a.m. I thought to myself, *Okay. If I get there really early, I can get in and get out in time to get to Bible study at church at 9:00.*

So I showed up at 7:00, assuming I would be bright and early and way ahead of everyone else. But I wasn't. I was dismayed to see a line of over two hundred people ahead of me, waiting at the door. I stood until the latest possible moment I could wait in line, with my face pressed against the glass, looking at that beautiful silk dress with the $40 price tag, designed by this great Italian designer. At 9:00, they announced there was no more merchandise by that designer; they had completely sold out.

Did I give up? Oh, no! I went home and looked up the dress on eBay, feeling like I *had* to have it.

And now I have it.

But was it worth it? Was it worth all of that effort and stress? Was it worth the investment of hours, waiting in line for the store to open? Nah, it's just squished between other hanging stuff in my already bulging closet.

We all have things that control our hearts from time to time. Hopefully we don't go too far down that road because Jonah had it right: "Those who cling to worthless idols forfeit the grace that could be theirs."

As John Calvin put it, the human heart is a perpetual "factory of idols."

Granted, some idols are less dysfunctional than others. You might say, "Well, at least I'm not a heroin addict. I've never been controlled by *that*." But maybe it's your career that saps all your energy and attention. Maybe it's the scramble for money. Maybe it's that house on the hill you've been dreaming about—to the point where you will sacrifice and strive for it more than for anything else. You will serve somebody. It is either-or: idols or the living God.

Yes, we agree with that. Yes, yes, yes of course! But here is the dilemma: How can we free ourselves from what so deeply entangles us and is imbedded in our fallen nature? Is it hopeless?

No!

Listen to Paul's heartfelt cry in Romans 7: "Oh, what a miserable person I am! Who will free me from this life that is dominated by sin and death? Thank God! The answer is in Jesus Christ our Lord" (verses 24-25, NLT).

Just as we looked to Him to save us, we can look to Him to change us! If He has the power to do one, He also has the power to do the other.

44: CHASING DOWN GENTLENESS

The fruit of the Spirit is . . . gentleness.

(GALATIANS 5:22-23)

Be beautiful inside, in your hearts, with the lasting
charm of a gentle and quiet spirit which is so
precious to God.

(1 PETER 3:4, TLB)

No sooner had I finished reading these verses the other morning when something came out of my mouth that did *not* represent the quiet and gentle spirit I've been hoping to cultivate. (I'll spare you the details.)

Immediately, I felt the loving stab of conviction. In my heart I whispered, *Lord, I'm sorry . . . again.*

We are told in 1 Timothy 6:11 that we must pursue gentleness. The word *pursue* is from a Greek word that could be translated "to run swiftly after, to press on and not be deterred in order to catch something." How easily we give up when we don't see changes in our lives overnight.

The transformation of a Christian's life is not "presto change-o," as if suddenly by magic. It is the longer, daily discipline of repentance and faith — daily taking up Jesus' yoke and learning from the One who was gentle and lowly.

So don't give up and give in to discouragement! Spiritual

change is a slow process that we must pursue day by day . . . and sometimes even moment by moment.

45: YOUR FINELY TUNED UNIVERSE

I will walk about in freedom, for I have sought out
your precepts.

(PSALM 119:45, NIV)

Not long ago, I heard a physicist make the statement that we
live in a finely tuned universe.

This is entirely in step with what the Bible teaches us.
In this universe, this reality in which we live out our lives, there
are rules. God Himself gave us those rules, those parameters,
because no one understands how this finely tuned universe
works better than He does, as its Designer and Creator.

He isn't just saying, "Hey, I'm the Boss, and I'm going to
throw down some rules just to let you know Who's in control
around here."

For instance, He doesn't say, "Here's an arbitrary command-
ment that you'd better obey: No matter how many times you are
offended, you are to forgive. So that's My rule, and you'd better
obey it."

No, that is not why He gives us this supernatural principle.
It's because He designed the human mind, He designed human
psychology, and He knows how unforgiveness leads to bitterness,
which poisons the mind and heart.

True freedom always operates under rules. In Psalm 119 the
psalmist writes, "To all perfection I see a limit; but your

commands are boundless" (verse 96, NIV).

In other words, "There is no limit to the freedom I experience when I am walking in Your will, staying on Your path, and following Your commands." Earlier on, he wrote this: "I will walk about in freedom, for I have sought out your precepts" (verse 45, NIV).

The psalmist isn't saying, "I relinquish my freedom and hamstring my life in order to serve You." No, he is saying, "Because I sought Your precepts, I walk at liberty."

Again, he is not saying, "I can't smoke and drink and run around because I have decided I am going to follow Your precepts." That isn't his perspective. His perspective is, "I am following Your precepts and commandments because in those I find myself walking in a broad, spacious place in great freedom. None of these earthly attractions will have a hold on me when I am living under Your righteous reign and rule in my life."

This is yet another amazing paradox: Where God is the master of your life, service to Him is perfect freedom.

His rules are *gracious* rules, given to us because He knows us and loves us. He says, "Don't commit adultery," "Don't have other gods before Me," and "Honor your father and mother" because He knows we can't be happy or fulfilled or even survive if we flout these laws.

When we violate His commands, whether "large" or "small," we harm ourselves and others. Maybe someone would say, "I can lie a bit, cheat a little here and there, talk behind someone's back, or blah, blah, blah. . . . It won't hurt anyone. Nothing will come of this."

But God knows that all sin, even "small" sin, is like tampering with the dials in that finely tuned universe that is your life. You begin to violate the structure of your own inner being, and many things—including some very large, very important, incredibly precious things—will be affected by your decision to indulge yourself in that sin.

What's more, you lose that indescribable sense of lightness and joy the psalmist wrote about: "I will walk about in freedom, for I have sought out your precepts."

I don't want to give that up. The price for whatever I want outside of His will is way too high.

46: DO THE NEXT THING

Jesus said to him, "Rise, take up your bed and walk."

(JOHN 5:8)

What do you do when you find yourself in a spiritual fog? I recommend Jesus' words in John 5: "Rise, take up your bed and walk."

My eyes fluttered open this morning in early November to the stillness that accompanied the grey fog. The only sound was the occasional drip-drop of water from the eaves onto the soggy ground. Outside my window, the house across the street was barely visible. No sign of sun. Underneath the olive tree, small beads of water collected on a spider's web, revealing the lacy design that hung suspended and drooping in the air.

These low clouds blanketed more than just the things I saw; they muffled the noises that normally stirred me awake. *Where are the birds this morning?* I wondered. *Are they still lingering in their warm nests like me?*

There are seasons of the soul as surely as there are seasons of the heart. And today the weather and my heart mirrored one another. What good comes from a season like this one? Grey inertia seems to be creeping through the neighborhood of my spiritual landscape. Over one year ago, in brilliant daylight, I knew such joy in loving and serving the Lord, which seemed almost effortless.

But now, in this fog, in this "in between-ness," I feel like I'm locked in limbo — caught in this lingering moment of time and space that is not quite pain, not quite pleasure. How do I progress spiritually in such a condition?

I've learned that if you project light directly into the fog, it simply bounces off the fog droplets and reflects in all directions, making it even harder to see. What normally works on a clear, dark night won't work in the fog. But did you know that fog tends to hover about twelve to eighteen inches off the ground, and that by projecting light into that fog-free pocket, you can illuminate the road a greater distance and see farther ahead?

I need to find my spiritual low beam lights and shine them straight out at bumper level and down, but not higher. Slowing down is so hard to do. But then, if I hadn't slowed down, I would have missed the jeweled spider web today. The best course for me today is to keep my expectations in check, keep my eyes on the path immediately in front of me, and not rush beyond what the light can reveal. I go to the Word of God, strike the match, and light the low beam lamp.

At a retreat many years ago I heard Elisabeth Elliot say, "When you don't know what to do next, simply do the next thing." If today, dear one, you are slowed and silenced in the fog, know God's will is not further beyond the light His Word can reveal to you today. Moment by moment, He will give us grace for the next step. So, make that cup of coffee, open the Word, and hear Him speak. And of course, the "next thing" for me is as simple as unloading the dishwasher and folding the laundry.

Here is the poem that includes the line I heard Elisabeth Elliot quote:

From an old English parsonage
    Down by the sea,
There came in the twilight
    A message to me.
Its quaint Saxon legend,
    Deeply engraven,
Hath as it seems to me,
    Teaching from Heaven;
And through the hours,
    The quiet words sing
Like a low inspiration,
    "Do the next thing."

Do it immediately,
    Do it with prayer;
Do it reliantly,
    Casting off care;
Do it with reverence,
    Tracing His hand,
Who hath placed it before thee
    With earnest command.
Stayed on Omnipotence,
    Safe 'neath His wing,
Leave all resultings —
    "Do the next thing."

Looking to Jesus,
    Ever serener,
Working or suffering,
    Be thy demeanor.
In the shade of His presence,
    The rest of His calm,

The light of His countenance,
Live out thy psalm,
Strong in His faithfulness,
Praise Him and sing:
Then, as He beckons thee,
"Do the next thing."

47: LOVE AND FREEDOM

Unless Your law had not been my delight, I would
then have perished in my affliction. . . . Oh, how I
love Your law! It is my meditation all the
day. . . . How sweet are Your words to my taste,
sweeter than honey to my mouth!

(PSALM 119:92,97,103)

In the ancient world, honey was the sweetest known substance.
To people living in that culture, honey was a once-in-a-year
delicacy treat and highly prized. That is how precious this relationship was—not just between the psalmist and the Bible, but
between the psalmist and the Lord of the Bible.

When you really love someone, aren't you willing to give up
a lot of things in order to know that person?

If you are married, think about when you first met your
husband. Didn't you go out of your way to find out everything
you could about him? What were his joys, his sorrows, his likes,
and his dislikes? Didn't you want to know what appealed to
him and what turned him off? Weren't you willing to take a
little time and think about those things? Of course you were.

Before you met that individual, you were free—free to go
where you wanted, choose what you wished, and do what you
liked. Maybe at some point in your relationship, you decided you
needed some alone time. You decided that you would get away

for the afternoon, have lunch with your girlfriends, and visit some of your old favorite stores where you liked to browse and shop. Maybe you just did this on an impulse, without ever telling your boyfriend or fiancé.

Back before cell phones and e-mails — and even before voice mail — you really could disappear for a few hours. But then sometime that evening you'd get a phone call: "Where were you? I couldn't reach you. I didn't know where you'd gone."

Maybe at that point it dawned on you: *I'm not as free as I was before I met him, but . . . it's kind of nice having someone who is concerned about me.* You begin to consider the fact that your relationship has progressed to a point that you have some obligations to this person. You can't just do whatever you feel like doing.

Okay, so now I am married to this person, and there are all kinds of things in my life where I have to bend my will his way. Why? Because he is the big bully, the man of the house and the authority, and he is laying down rules in my life?

No, not really.

It's because I love him and care about him and value our marriage. I think more about him than I do violating some "rule." When Greg wants to meet me for lunch in half an hour, I know that he means a little bit sooner than half an hour. For him, being "on time" is late, and being late is simply unacceptable. If I show up thirty seconds late, he's looking at his watch.

Now, I will admit that those are more his values than my values, and I have struggled with how he makes a big deal out of being precisely on time for everything. And yet I know that (for whatever reason) it is really important to Greg, so I try to adapt to that.

But he has to adapt, too.

When we watch some adaptation of a Dickens novel in a BBC production, I know that he has very little interest whatsoever in those kinds of shows. Nevertheless, he watches them with me (most of the time he dozes on and off, but at least he is with me while I watch). Why is he doing that when he could be doing something else he enjoys more? Is it because he feels obligated to restrict his freedom in this instance? No, he does it because he knows it makes me happy.

The nature of true love is a willingness to live under restrictions because we want—we truly desire—to please that person. That alone explains the somewhat odd language that we encounter in Psalm 119.

Dr. Martyn Lloyd-Jones said, "Love is not just a sentiment. Love is a great controlling passion, and it always expresses itself in terms of obedience."

Just think about what happens when you fall in love. Most of us begin to make little mental notes about that person. You are looking for hints about them. You want to know who their friends are, what hobbies they have, what they like to eat. And if the relationship is growing, you inevitably discover your behavior and your interests beginning to fall in line with their behavior and interests. You find you start to like musicals and mountain biking and sushi too—things you may never have liked before!

The psalmist does what he does out of love for the Lord and His Word. He is willing to conform to what he knows of the Lord: loving what He loves and hating what He hates. Jesus spoke of the same dynamic in John 14:23, where He said, "If anyone loves Me, he will keep My word; and My Father will love him, and We will come to him and make Our home with him."

Jesus isn't saying, "If you obey Me, I will love you." (Thank goodness! None of us would be loved if that were true.) No, He is saying, "If you love Me, *you will obey Me.*" The emphasis is on love. This is the supreme motivation for coming under God's authority.

"If you love Me . . ."

What an incredible appeal and invitation. He is saying, "If

you love Me, come My way. It will fulfill you. I know you so well, and I know that this will bring you true happiness. In the long run, My rules are for your good."

Then He says, "And My Father and I will come to you and make Our home with you." What a precious and intimate thought, coming from the God of the universe!

48: EVERY GIRL KNOWS THE FEELING

I will praise You, for I am fearfully and
wonderfully made.

(PSALM 139:14)

"All of my will has always been to conquer some horrible feeling of inad-
equacy. I'm always struggling with that fear. I push past one spell of it
and discover myself as a special human being, and then I get to another
stage and think I'm mediocre and uninteresting.... That's always been
pushing me, pushing me. Because even though I have become somebody,
I still have to prove that I am SOMEBODY." —Madonna, in an interview with
Vogue[1]

Every girl knows the feeling. We want to feel loved. We want
to know we matter.

Despite all we may accomplish, there are lingering questions: *Who am I? Why am I here? Where do I go to find the answers?*

Science keeps telling us that we are the product of some
chance collision of protein and molecules that occurred billions
of years ago. We just happened. Human life is nothing more
than the result of a mutation of some single cell that just got
lucky.

Where do I come from? What am I? Where am I going?
Impressionist painter Paul Gauguin left France to find a paradise

of tropical beauty and went to Tahiti with all its promise of sunlight and freedom. Sadly, he was unable to find what it was he was searching for.

One day, after finishing what some consider his greatest masterpiece, he took a bottle of arsenic, walked into the mountains, and killed himself. The title he had given his painting contained the very questions he never could answer: *D'où Venons Nous / Que Sommes Nous / Où Allons,* which translates to "Where do we come from? What are we? Where are we going?"

We're given the answers in God's Word. You were not only divinely designed, but you were designed for a purpose. We are God's *haute couture*. The term is French for "high sewing" — the creation of exclusive, one-of-a-kind, custom-fitted clothing for a specific customer.

In fact, we are created in the image of God Himself. He made us and formed us with care and breathed into us being. We didn't just happen. The Bible tells who we are and how we can live meaningful lives in Him.

This fact should give us a great sense of significance and belonging, regardless of how others make you feel. No one needs to ever feel fearful or unloved. Your fingerprints and DNA are like no one else's who has ever lived. God fashioned you intricately in your mother's womb:

> You formed my inward parts;
> You covered me in my mother's womb. . . .
> I am fearfully and wonderfully made. . . .
> My frame was not hidden from You,
> When I was made in secret,
> And skillfully wrought in the lowest parts of the earth.
> Your eyes saw my substance, being yet unformed. (Psalm 139:13-16)

God organized that unseen substance that makes you, and you are more than just forty-six chromosomes or blueprints. Science is sounding more and more like religion when it tells us that our DNA is not just the paper and ink that makes the book of our lives. Our DNA conveys information that is so complex and so vast that it is compared to a language.

If it is a language, then who is the author? The denial of God as the One who formed us is like reading Shakespeare's plays and not believing there's a playwright. How foolish that would be! There must be an Author because His signature is all over creation. There must be a Designer. Just look in the mirror!

You won't learn this in your biology class. You won't read it in *Cosmopolitan,* and your girlfriends—unless they're believers—aren't going to have a clue.

These truths from God's Word give us a confidence that can't be obtained anywhere else in all the world. They not only keep us on the right course, but they will lead us to that path of significance we are all searching for—a life that will have significance not only for now, but for all eternity.

49: HONEST TO GOD

"If you have run with the footmen, and they have wearied you, then how can you contend with horses?"

(JEREMIAH 12:5)

When we get into a Bible study, we might enjoy looking up cross-references, chasing down the meaning of Greek or Hebrew words, trying to understand the context of various passages, and so on. When we do, we say we are "searching the Bible."

But we also need to let the Bible search us.

We aren't just looking to fill our heads with facts and figures; we're opening ourselves up to a dialogue with God, through His Holy Spirit. So we let the Scriptures talk to us as we read and ponder. We let the Word debate with us, argue with us, convict us, challenge us, and even scold us.

I love reading the prophet Jeremiah, because as he is faithful to speak the words of the Lord even when his life is at risk, he is also honest enough to reveal his own fears and struggles. He's a volatile, emotional prophet. One minute he is declaring these incredibly bold proclamations, and the next minute his eyes are a fountain of tears. Then in other places he says, "God, this is so *hard*! I wish I had never been born!"

Do you know what the Lord says to him? Here is how it reads in *The Message*:

"So, Jeremiah, if you're worn out in this footrace with men,
what makes you think you can race against horses?
And if you can't keep your wits during times of calm,
what's going to happen when troubles break loose
like the Jordan in flood?" (Jeremiah 12:5)

Jeremiah was in a tough place. He was a lonely voice crying in the wilderness, and even his family had forsaken him. He had been rejected, humiliated, roughed up, and jailed in solitary confinement . . . in mud . . . up to his armpits. We can understand how this servant of God might complain a little. But the Word of God came to him and challenged him, saying, in effect, "Buck up, Jeremiah. It isn't going to get easier. In fact, it may be harder. You'd better strengthen yourself in Me."

This is what the Word of God does in our lives.

Sometimes when I am whining and complaining, God's Word will come to me and say, "Stop it, Cathe. Stop your complaining. You need to turn your complaints into praises, because you know I am in control here and want your best."

That is what you want when you go to the Scriptures. You don't want to walk away from the Word of God unmoved and unchanged. You *want* to be convicted. You *want* your heart to be transformed. Martin Luther once said, "The Bible is alive, it speaks to me; it has feet, it runs after me; it has hands, it lays hold of me."[1]

We need to come under the scrutiny of God's Word, allowing it to soothe us or shake us, challenge us or calm our anxious hearts.

The shepherd in ancient Israel might very well have used his rod to crack and break a leg on a sheep that continually wandered away and put itself in danger. But he would also take that rod and run it over the wooly nap of the sheep to search for any pests or parasites that might have burrowed down into the sheep's skin. And then he would lovingly and patiently remove them.

That is what the Word of God does. It searches our lives, removing those things that are hurtful and harmful to us.

King David said it best when he prayed,

Search me, O God, and know my heart;
Try me, and know my anxieties;
And see if there is any wicked way in me,
And lead me in the way everlasting. (Psalm 139:23-24)

We need to be open to and honest with God . . . then carefully and prayerfully listen to what He challenges us to do next.

50: WISE OR ... OTHERWISE?

If you need wisdom, ask our generous God, and he
will give it to you. He will not rebuke you for
asking.

(James 1:5, nlt)

We girls, wives, and mothers need wisdom! Making decisions about friends, hobbies, marriage, careers, school, money—you name it—we need God's wisdom to discern in matters great and small . . . to see what isn't always apparent.

When faced with obvious difficulties and dangers, we'll certainly cry out to God for His help. So we should! We are prone to succumb to fear and worry, and our weaknesses and limitations drive us to our knees.

But in some situations, when we feel confident to handle things, we fail to ask God for wisdom. After all, most of us have at least a few human resources we can rely on.

This is where Joshua 9 serves as such a stark reminder to us. After the Israelites' victories over the cities of Jericho and Ai, they were approached by men who wanted to make a peace agreement with them. They knew better. The Lord had given them specific instructions not to enter into any agreement with foreigners. But because these men appeared to have come from a very far country, it seemed safe enough. They failed to inquire of the Lord and made a huge mistake by entering into a treaty with them.

We, like the children of Israel, may have the courage to withstand an obvious enemy attack, but do we have the sense to detect deception? Things may not be as innocent as they appear.

Do you live each day in humble dependence on God to be a wise woman? Failure to inquire of the Lord has led many to make disastrous choices. The apostle James asked his flock in James 3:13, "Who is wise and understanding among you?"

The answer?

No one is wise enough, by herself, to live and choose correctly — only the woman who knows she needs God's help . . . in everything.

How do we safeguard ourselves and our families? We must humbly seek God, search the Scriptures, and ask for the wisdom He has graciously promised to give (see Joshua 9; James 1:5; 3:13).

51: GIRLS KNOW HOW TO CHARM

The fear of the LORD is the beginning of wisdom; a good understanding have all those who do His commandments. His praise endures forever.

(PSALM 111:10)

apa, Papa," she begins to cry. "I don't want to take a nap."

Her words have that sweet, persuasive emphasis on "Paaa-Paaa" as she looks lovingly at him, her big, blue eyes filling with tears.

I must admit, we girls certainly know how to turn on the charm. No one has to teach us this. It is inherent in little girls—along with sugar and spice and everything nice.

My granddaughter Stella already knows just how to charm her papa. And would you believe it? It works every time.

In Proverbs 31:30 we read, "Charm is deceptive, and beauty is fleeting; but a woman who fears the LORD is to be praised" (NIV). I read this as a warning about how we women can use our wiles to get our way.

Sometimes, we are certain that our way is the best way. I have "been there, done that" myself—certain I am right about how, when, what, or where something is to be done. Then, down the road after I get my way, I am forced to realize just how little I really know.

My wisdom is based only on information I have processed.

By definition, then, my wisdom is limited because my knowledge is limited. All too often, I don't have all I need to make a wise decision. Why do I go ahead anyway? Because my heart is often led astray by my own desires for a simple, quick, and painless solution.

Someone wisely said that beauty fades, but dumb is forever. God help us to not be dumb! What may seem good in the short term may be disastrous in the long run.

So where do we get this wisdom we need for life? Psalm 111:10 tells us, "The fear of the LORD is the beginning of wisdom."

What is the fear of the Lord? Many are confused and misunderstand what this means. Fear is often associated with that knot in the stomach, that sinking, heart-pounding, often paralyzing emotion. Is this the fear we are to have for the Lord? Is it the same fear as the fear of falling off a cliff or facing a wild animal?

The other day, while leaving the shopping center, Greg and I bumped into a friend who is a chief of police. As we stood there talking together, it was interesting to watch how people changed as soon as they noticed this man in uniform.

Those who drove by took notice of him and slowed way down. People on the sidewalk deferred to him, all because of his uniform and what it represents. He has the authority to write them a ticket, or even arrest them. That's certainly a type of fear.

A few days later, I happened to see him at church with his three beautiful daughters. I watched them as they held his hand and leaned close to his shoulder, expressing their affection.

Now, I'm sure they fear their father, but it is not because they dread what he might do to them. This fear of their father is out of love. There is respect, not the terror some may feel toward an officer of the law. No, their fear is one based on relationship and love; they would not want to hurt or disappoint him.

Theologians have made the distinction between *servile* fear and *filial* fear. The Latin root of *servile* is from the same word as slave, while *filial* is from the Latin root for child.

A slave knows nothing of the affection and privilege a child feels for his loving parent. Servile fear is essentially a self-centered fear, fear of what can happen to us, a fear of punishment.

Filial fear is entirely different. Filial fear is a respect and reverence that wants to avoid causing any kind of hurt.

A woman who fears the Lord is not afraid of God, but only wants to please Him. Why? Because she loves Him.

So here is where we begin our quest for the virtuous life. *And it isn't a list of dos and don'ts.* Some of us just love lists, don't we? We love the ability to cross things off or check each box. It gives such a sense of accomplishment and pride.

But here is where we must be very careful. It's possible to do many things—even good things—with our lives. And so we should. But is that all the Lord requires? No, He is far more interested in the motives of our hearts.

Augustine said that the key to life change is not the act of the will, but the loves of the heart. If we're not careful to first tend to the loves of our hearts, we will easily slip back into that slavelike fear.

That is why we are told in Proverbs 4:23, "Above all else, guard your heart, for it is the wellspring of life" (NIV).

You might begin today with a prayer something like this: *Lord, You know all things. You see every facet of my life—my hopes as well as my fears. It is my desire to live a life that is pleasing to You, for only then will I have a life worth living. Take all my heart and fill me with that loving, childlike fear so I might learn to be wise. Thank You, Father, for loving me for Jesus' sake. Amen.*

52: "HOLD THEM LOOSELY"

"People are like grass; their beauty is like a flower in the field."

(1 PETER 1:24, NLT)

Not long ago I looked at our wedding pictures and thought to myself, *Yes, we are fading. The hair is fading. So is the eyesight, hearing, and even our memories.*

The other day when I was standing in the bathroom, getting ready, I said to Greg, "It's just so sad how . . ."

"Yes?" he said, waiting for me to finish my thought.

There was a short pause, and I said, "I don't know! I totally forgot what I was talking about!"

It seems so weird sometimes. You walk into a room to get something, and then you simply can't remember what you were looking for. You stand there looking around, knowing that you wanted something, but what it might have been escapes you.

Teasing me about my memory lapse, Greg said to me, "This is really sad, Cathe. You're in the *middle of a sentence* and you can't remember what you are saying. You'll have to start writing down notes so you can remember what to say to me."

I read an article that spoke of how women at a certain age have to embrace the fact that "they have more dimension in their faces." Dimension! What a nice way to describe sags and wrinkles.

In 1 Peter, the apostle writes, "People are like grass; their beauty is like a flower in the field. The grass withers and the flower fades. But the word of the Lord remains forever"

(1:24-25, NLT). The truth is, if you live long enough, you will lose everything that is tangible. Sooner or later, life will disappoint you. Sooner or later, many of your earthly hopes will fade. And trust me, it will help if you keep a sense of humor as you age and see your body changing.

A few years ago in Dallas, we had a wonderful barbecue lunch with Chuck Swindoll. As we sat, munching on chips and queso dip, he said to us with a tear in his eye, "Hold everything loosely. *Hold it loosely.*"

Chuck actually was quoting something Corrie ten Boom (who survived the concentration camps in World War II) said to him when he was a young pastor. He told us how he had been shaking hands in the foyer one Sunday morning, greeting his parishioners, when she approached him. Noticing the children standing at his side, she asked in that unmistakable Dutch accent, "Are these yours?"

"Yes," he beamed.

She then gave him the warning that only a woman who has lived a long time and walked a long way with the Lord has the clout to give: "Hold them loosely. Hug them tightly, but hold them loosely. Because it will hurt very much if the Father has to pry them from your fingers."

Chuck looked both of us directly in the eyes and said, "I have tried to do that."

How could he have known that in a short time, we would have to open our hands, loosen our grip, and trust the Lord to watch over our son Christopher?

It's good counsel concerning our loved ones. Be thankful for them. Enjoy them. Love them. Hug them. Kiss them. But remember to hold them loosely because this world and everyone in it will pass away.

That is why we need a living hope—a hope that suffering and death cannot, and never will, destroy.

53: DRIVEN INTO JOY

These [trials] have come so that your faith — of
greater worth than gold, which perishes even
though refined by fire — may be proved genuine
and may result in praise, glory and honor when
Jesus Christ is revealed.

(1 Peter 1:7, niv)

It has been cold in Southern California this week. Last night I
had a restless night — I didn't sleep well at all, and I could hear
the heater kicking on and off, on and off. It reminded me of a
statement I heard once: "Sorrow doesn't destroy true joy, *it turns
it up*. It's like seeing the stars shine brighter and sharper, like
gemstones, as the sky grows darker and darker at night."

That is how hope will work in our lives . . . if we let it. Like
the cold at night that triggers the heater to turn on in our house,
sorrow, mysterious as it may seem, can trigger joy in our hearts.
Joy that is deeper and more unshakable than we have ever
experienced.

What happens when you put gold into a furnace? Does it
burn up? No. It just gets brighter. As C. S. Lewis wrote in *A
Grief Observed*, "God has not been trying an experiment on my
faith or love in order to find out their quality. He knew it already.
It was I who didn't."[1]

I always thought this verse in 1 Peter meant that we will

praise, glory, and honor Christ at His return, and of course we will, but that's not all Peter is saying here. He is saying that grief, sorrow, and fiery trials will result in praise and glory and honor *in your life*. We will one day hear Christ say to us, "Well done, good and faithful servant."

If that reassurance doesn't bring you joy, I don't know what will.

This passage is saying that in the very midst of your trial, be it large or small, you can have a taste of the Lord's praise, glory, and honor as you suffer faithfully and joyfully in whatever it is you are facing.

Paul speaks about this concept in 2 Corinthians 4:17: "For our light affliction, which is but for a moment, is working for us a far more exceeding and eternal weight of glory."

I have seen it in the faces of people who are in extreme suffering—believers who are trusting the Lord even as they endure horrific times. I have seen a radiance in their faces when everything that would seemingly bring a person happiness, joy, or peace has been stripped away. It is something that bubbles out of the depths, clear, sparkling, radiant. And it makes no earthly sense at all. The affliction you endure right now is working in you a weight of glory that you can't obtain in any other way. How awesome to think that He would share His resplendent, magnificent, incomparable glory with us as we suffer joyfully, keeping our eyes fixed on Him.

As you go through trials, you will begin to catch a glimpse of what God is doing—working something in your life that is glorious and beautiful beyond description.

If you have the living hope that Peter writes about, sorrow actually can drive you deeper into Jesus, *and that drives you into joy.*

54: GOD, THE GREAT ALCHEMIST

For I consider that the sufferings of this present
time are not worthy to be compared with the glory
which shall be revealed in us.

(ROMANS 8:18)

As I write these words, it has been one year since my son
Christopher died in a traffic accident. That's 365 days . . .
8,760 hours . . . 525,600 minutes. David once wrote to the
Lord, "You . . . put my tears into Your bottle; are they not in
Your book?" (Psalm 56:8).

How many tears are in that bottle now?

I want to say up front, I don't like this. Losing a loved one is
more painful than I ever imagined it would be. To me, it has
made no sense. Why did his fragile computer survive the crash
and light up instantly—and yet Christopher was gone? Apple
could produce an ad based on the durability and resilience of
their product . . . but I just want my son back, here with me.

Nevertheless, I cannot change what happened on the 91
freeway that July morning. So I don't ask why anymore.

I am certain that God never wastes a hurt, so I have often
wondered, *Will all this sadness and pain and loss somehow be transformed into much greater joy when we arrive in heaven?*

In the Middle Ages, there were men called alchemists who
tried to transform common lead into gold. They spent their days

trying to discover that essential missing ingredient, the mystical key that would make this possible. Try as they might, they always came up unsuccessful.

I try to add it all up, walk around and around the tragedy of Christopher's death, look at it from all sides, and reason it out as best I can. At times, with eyes of faith, I can see a divine plan so clearly, and yes, I can even rejoice. Our faith is, after all, the religion of the Cross. As suffering was the Savior's path to glory, we, too, are transformed on that path. The God who counts our tears doesn't want to waste our tears.

Yet honestly, at other times I am swallowed by immense waves of grief and unanswered questions, and I am left perplexed. Like Paul, I am "perplexed, but not in despair" (2 Corinthians 4:8).

The Greek word for *perplexed* carries the notion that temporarily we are "in straits, left wondering why and longing." This year has not been a cakewalk, but we are not in despair. We absolutely are not utterly despairing or without hope.

So I go back to my original question: Will all this sadness and pain somehow be transformed into something far, far better?

Paul wrote to his friends in Rome about his own suffering and said, "For I consider that the sufferings of this present time are not worthy to be compared with the glory which shall be revealed in us" (Romans 8:18). He considered, reasoned, and concluded that all that is endured for Christ would one day look so small when compared to the glory and beauty that awaits us.

Therefore, I must add it all up and reason it out in light of His Word and not my own understanding.

Paul's statement tells me that God is the Great Alchemist. He takes the ugly and hard troubles that we suffer and turns them into things of extreme value, far greater than even gold. As Paul writes in 2 Corinthians 4:17, "For our light and momentary troubles are achieving for us an eternal glory that far outweighs them all" (NIV).

In heaven's economy, we are trading lead for gold. So I will relinquish to God the base metal of my life, my hopes for happiness, and specifically, the future as I dreamed it would be—to watch my son Christopher grow old with his wife and children in a home of their own—and surrender to the Great Alchemist.

> Be still, my soul: thy Jesus can repay
> From His own fullness all He takes away.[1]

55: BELIEVE, AND GO ON BELIEVING

> But the soul of my lord shall be bound in the
> bundle of life with the LORD thy God; and the souls
> of thine enemies, them shall he sling out, as out of
> the middle of a sling.
>
> (1 SAMUEL 25:29, KJV)

I was telling my granddaughter Stella a Bible story the other day.

She said to me, "I already heard that story."

Stella may have heard it, but she certainly didn't understand it completely. None of us has. Life—eternal life—is a matter of knowing the gospel, but not like you know your multiplication tables. It is a matter of believing the gospel . . . and then going right on believing in that gospel every day of our lives.

Yes, I believed the gospel and received salvation from Christ in 1972. But I also believe the gospel every day of my life. It is what shapes me. It is what keeps me going, taking the next step, facing the challenges of each new day. I find the hope to live my life. Hope comes by believing the gospel.

My mom is a Roman Catholic. A few years ago she got herself a Bible and announced that she was going to read it through, cover to cover. And she did! I was so proud of her. As a result, we had some amazing conversations about things she had never read or realized the Bible said. I remember her asking me,

"Who was Melchizedek?" She was so fascinated by that story in the Old Testament.

Just recently my sister Mary asked her, "Mom, are you still reading your Bible?"

"No," she answered, "I already read it."

What some of us don't understand is that the story is new every time you open it. You can never get to the bottom of the well; you can always go deeper and deeper, and fresh meaning bubbles up to the surface every time you read it.

First Peter 1:12 tells us that the Good News is so rich and deep and profound that "even angels long to look into these things" (NIV). That Greek word translated "long" in this verse means a hyperdesire, a craving, a hunger that is never satisfied. That is how the angels in heaven desire to understand more about the gospel message. It reminds me that if these intelligent, immortal, glorious, sinless beings hunger to learn more and more about the gospel message, how much more should we believe it and keep looking into it?

And here is something else we should never tire of thinking about: Peter reminds us that we have "an inheritance that can never perish, spoil or fade—kept in heaven for you" (1 Peter 1:4, NIV). You and I have a legacy, an inheritance beyond our wildest dreams. It's almost as if Peter can't come up with enough words to describe it. *Unfading. Undying. Incorruptible. Kept and preserved in heaven for you.*

A few days ago I went out for a jog, taking with me the key I needed to get back into my house. I had taken it off the keychain, because it was too clumsy to jog with my iPod and a wad of keys. But what should I do with the key? I didn't want to hold it in my hand and possibly drop it along the way.

I decided to put it in a safe place. I tucked it away in my clothing and began my run. Halfway around my course I suddenly asked myself, *Where is that key?* I must have looked just a little bit strange to the other joggers as I gave myself a pat down. Did I put it in my leggings? Did it slip out along the way? Then I suddenly remembered: I had tucked it into my shoe. I reached down and found it, feeling a little flood of relief as I did. I didn't have to go running through the wilderness forever. I could get back into the house now.

Just as I had taken that key and put it in a safe place where it wouldn't be lost or fall out, so our lives, our hope, our future is safe. It is bound in the bundle of life with the Lord our God. We have His Word on it, His promise. And it is a living hope. Back at home, I was reminded of something that the young warrior David was told by a very wise woman named Abigail when he was being persecuted and chased around the country by the jealous King Saul. She reminded him of something he had forgotten.

In this particular incident, he was on the cusp of making a very bad decision, taking some rash action because he was angry and had lost his perspective on the situation. Abigail came to him and basically said, "Don't take that rash action." And then she reminded him, "A man is risen to pursue thee, and to seek thy soul: but the soul of my lord shall be bound in the bundle of life with the Lord thy God" (1 Samuel 25:29, kjv).

Tap into that hope today, no matter what your life situation might be. Remember, your very life is bound up in Him.

56: THE FRUIT OF A THOUSAND CHOICES

Put your hope in God, for I will yet praise him, my
Savior and my God.

(PSALM 42:11, NIV)

We want to know: How is it possible to be thankful and praise God for the things we cannot comprehend? The psalmists show us the way.

The book of Psalms gives us permission to ask why, how, when. In one psalm, David cries out, "Awake, O Lord! Why do you sleep?" (44:23, NIV). I love the honesty, the rawness of his prayer. He didn't tidy it up to impress us. He bares his soul so freely, confident his God will understand. We are in good company; there are many others in Scripture who knew tears as their food day and night (see Psalm 42:3). After all, the Lord Jesus Christ Himself called from His cross, "My God, My God, why . . . ?"

I read in Psalm 42, couched in the midst of the cries and questions, of a tremendous strength. One moment the psalmist pours out his soul to God, and the next he preaches to himself:

Why are you downcast, O my soul?
    Why so disturbed within me?
Put your hope in God,
    for I will yet praise him,
    my Savior and my God. (verse 11, NIV)

I will yet praise Him! This is the final verse in the psalm. There was no quick fix, no answer on the horizon. His condition hadn't changed. But despite his bewilderment, he determined to praise his Savior and God.

Is this some form of holy schizophrenia? Perhaps, but I can assure you that God is in favor of this kind of self-talk. We must learn how to preach to our own hearts in tough times.

Greg, when being hit with thoughts of doubt, has used these words: "Greg, shut up!" Strong words, I know, but whatever words you choose, you must urge yourself to do more than rehearse your painful situation. Command your heart into obedience and put your hope in God, who is worthy of our praise.

Maybe with broken hearts, tear-stained faces, and voices hoarse from crying, we can rise above our circumstances and offer thanks, a sacrifice of praise.

Why should we do this? Because (and let's face it) either we believe God is good and is in control, or we had better quit the charade, pack our bags, and call it a day. Instead, I pray that you will join me and many others who continue to believe and give thanks, in spite of how we feel and what we face.

As Nancy Leigh DeMoss wrote, "The grateful heart that springs forth in joy is not acquired in a moment; it is the fruit of a thousand choices."[1]

57: THE SECRET STOREHOUSE

In the year that King Uzziah died, I saw the Lord
sitting on a throne, high and lifted up, and the train
of His robe filled the temple.

(ISAIAH 6:1)

Early on in our marriage, Greg and I were as close to broke as
you can get. At times we were pretty desperate to come up
with the funds to pay our bills. Greg was being paid a whopping $75 a week. I distinctly remember when those first bills
came in the mail. I had just turned eighteen and had lived my
whole life in my father's house. I had never lived on my own, and
I had never looked at bills, thought about bills, or worried about
bills.

Then all of a sudden these bills started coming in the mail.
I looked at our water bill and thought, *You mean you have to pay
for* water? It was more my pride than faith in God that kept me
from calling my mom and dad and saying, "We are desperate.
Can you write us a check and loan us the money?" They hadn't
really wanted me to marry Greg, so if I had rejected their advice
about whom to marry, how could I go back and ask them to pay
for our water bill?

Do you know what I learned in those days?

I learned about Jehovah-jireh. I learned God was my
provider. And He came through! There were times when Greg

and I were in need, as the children of Israel had been in need. (There were also times when I learned we didn't need all the things we *thought* we needed.) But God came through for us in those days, and He has provided for me to this day. The Lord is our provider.

Do you realize that all of heaven's resources are at your disposal? God has a secret storehouse. But He doesn't bring all of the riches out at once; He brings them out as we need them. And there is no end or limit to His supply.

The children of Israel needed to learn this lesson in the wilderness wanderings. Instead of turning to this incomparable, all-powerful God who loved them, time after time they turned to Moses, the guy they could *see*. But Moses hadn't brought them through the Red Sea. Moses hadn't given them manna. Moses hadn't sweetened the undrinkable water at Mara. God had done all of that. And yet, when the crisis came, they turned to a man.

It's often that way with us. When trouble comes, we turn to our own friends and counselors. We turn to our rich uncle (or whomever) to meet the need of the moment and get us through the crisis. But do you know what? God wants to be our resource. He wants us to turn to Him for help.

To whom do you turn in a crisis? Are you tempted to pick up the phone, call your best friend, and go back over the same stuff again and again and lament and worry and complain? Do you run to the bank to see if you can procure an emergency loan?

Here's what I would suggest: Go to God *first*.

Look to the Lord, pour out your heart to Him, thank Him in advance for meeting your needs, and then wait on Him to act and to show you what to do.

There is a wonderful illustration of this in the book of Isaiah. In the sixth chapter, the prophet said, "In the year that King Uzziah died, I saw the Lord seated on a throne, high and exalted, and the train of his robe filled the temple" (verse 1, NIV). Some commentators point out that Uzziah actually was Isaiah's rich relative. He was a king, and it may be that whenever Isaiah had a need, he turned to Uzziah for provision. But then Uzziah died, and in *that* year, after those resources had dried up, Isaiah saw the glory of the Lord on a high throne. Isaiah had a vision of God like he had never seen before.

I don't want to miss an experience like that. I don't want to go running to someone else, to some human resource to try to meet my needs. I want to see His glory, don't you? I want a fresh vision of who He is and what He can do. And here is the amazing thing: God wants to show us His glory even more than we want to see it!

58: LITTLE LADY, WAKE UP!

But when Jesus heard it, He answered him, saying,
"Do not be afraid; only believe, and she will be
made well."

(LUKE 8:50)

I n Luke's gospel, we read the story of a man who certainly
thought Jesus was too late. As a matter of fact, his friends even
told him, "There's no use troubling the Teacher now."

Like a first-century 911 call, Jairus reached Jesus by falling
on his knees and begging attention for his only daughter, who
was twelve years old and dying of a fever. His only hope was
hanging by a single thread in the form of this young rabbi from
Galilee.

But as Jairus was hurrying Jesus back to his house, hoping it
wasn't going to be too late, a huge crowd was pushing and slowing the way, to the point of almost crushing them.

Suddenly, Jairus's plan was derailed when Jesus stopped and
asked, "Who touched Me?" Everyone denied it. And Peter said,
"Master, the multitudes throng and press You" (Luke 8:45). But
Jesus knew someone had touched the tassels of His garment and
that power had flowed out of Him.

In those agonizing moments of time, a nameless, destitute
woman had come from behind and cut in line, securing her healing. Jairus may have been thinking, *This woman, sick as she may*

be, would have lived another day. Why is Jesus stopping to speak to her now?

It's curious how easy it is to dismiss the needs of others as insignificant when we compare them to our own. So often we can't see beyond our own needs. And that is why Jesus' dealings were so often surprising—even disturbing—to everyone. It was the tax collectors, notorious sinners, leprosy stricken, and immoral women who reached His heart. He had as much concern for the nameless, insignificant, poor, and chronically sick woman as He had for this obviously "deserving" ruler of the synagogue.

For Jairus, how could he have known that both healing and resurrection were easily within Jesus' power? Would a resurrection have even entered his mind? Raising someone from the dead is so rare—even in Scripture. What Jesus was about to do for Jairus, then, was exceedingly abundantly above all he could ask or think! But all in His good time . . .

Jesus also knew He was not going to allow this woman to leave with just a quick fix for her physical problem. What she needed was an encounter that would pale in comparison to a healing. It would transform her from the inside out. She would hear the words, "Daughter, your faith has healed you. Go in peace and be freed from your suffering."

Why does God allow delays? I don't know all the answers to this question, especially when I am in the thick of a desperate situation, but there are a few principles that I can learn from the case of Jairus.

PEOPLE MATTER TO JESUS.

All kinds of people, not just the rich, influential, "good" folks. This woman was "unclean," destitute, and isolated, but despite how others looked at her, Jesus wouldn't risk losing her in the crowd. His compassion extended beyond a mere healing; He wanted to make sure she was set free from bondage and at peace with God. "Daughter, your faith has healed you. Go in peace and be freed from your suffering."

DELAYS ARE OFTEN HIS WAY OF KNOCKING THE SELF-CENTEREDNESS OUT OF OUR HEARTS.

How often I have prayed in recent years, *Lord Jesus, just come now! Take us all home. Isn't it about time?* Yet in the years that I have waited, how many more souls have been born into eternal life? In my selfish desire to be delivered, have I forgotten that God is exceedingly patient toward those I may not give a passing glance?

IN OUR WAITING PLACES, WE NEED TO SEE THE NEEDS OF OTHERS WE CAN TEND TO IN CHRIST'S NAME.

We can and should rejoice that in delays, we have more time to spread the Good News to as many people as we can!

WHAT LIES IN OUR FUTURE, BEYOND THE WAITING AND PAIN, IS OFTEN AN EVEN GREATER AND MORE GLORIOUS ANSWER THAN WE COULD IMAGINE.

Jairus would see Jesus' power displayed in such a tender and loving way. His little girl would have her touch from the Master in good time. We read Jesus' words, spoken gently, *Talitha koum*: "Little girl, arise" (Luke 8:54). Even in the worst-case scenario, death, our greatest enemy, isn't to be feared. In the end, it will have no power over the believer. It will be nothing more than a sweet night's sleep from which we will hear our Savior say, "Dear one, it is time to get up."

Can we trust Him when our time schedules are stretched to the limits and snapped? Jairus didn't know how this would end or that a resurrection would tap no more of Jesus' power than healing a fever. Jesus said to him, "Do not be afraid; only believe."

All who believe will hear their own "*Talitha koum.*"

59: RESTORATION

Therefore we do not lose heart. Even though our outward man is perishing, yet the inward man is being renewed day by day.

(2 CORINTHIANS 4:16)

Our first house, the first house Greg and I ever owned, was an old farmhouse in Riverside, California. We paid all of $38,000 for it.

The house looked okay when we bought it, but we were so mesmerized with the idea of owning our own home that we didn't really consider how old this place was or how much work it would take to maintain it.

It was what you might call a money pit.

Yes, it was a grand old Victorian wood farmhouse, but it had seen its day — years, probably decades, before.

We first got a sense of how old this house was when Greg's grandfather, whom we called "Daddy Charles," saw the antiquated light switch and exclaimed, "These are the kinds of light switches we had when I was a boy!"

One of the things I would say to anyone who wants to purchase a very old house is that it will take everything you've got. At some point, Greg and I realized that the house's restoration needs were going to be never-ending! Yes, it had some "beautiful bones," as the realtor put it, but you can't imagine how much work it turned out to be.

I think about our lives. Apart from the restoration work of the Holy Spirit, we are like that old Victorian house of ours. There is so much work to be done in our personalities and in our old habits that we might sometimes fear God will just scrap us, that He will leave the keys on the counter and walk away from us as a bad investment . . . a money pit. But He doesn't do that. He doesn't remove personalities or wipe out all our past memories.

No, He redeems and restores them.

There is such hope in that. He doesn't want to exchange your personality for a new one; He wants to redeem it. He wants to make you into the person He always intended you to be.

60: ALL MY SPRINGS

As well the singers as the players on instruments
shall be there: all my springs are in thee.

(PSALM 87:7, KJV)

When I was little, we had a *bodega*.

My Spanish mother kept good supplies of everything that was needed to run the house in that storeroom — all the bottles of vinegars and olive oils, tins of tuna, and bags of rice. Everything that was needed, she would store up. My dad would laugh and complain that years after they were gone, we would have enough of her favorite cologne to scent the sheets for generations!

In Psalm 87:7, the psalmist writes, "All my springs are in thee" (KJV). Can you affirm that all your resources, all that you really have need of, all the most important things in life and eternity, are found in Him? Are your springs found in Him? God has a secret storehouse, with provision beyond your conception. As the old hymn affirms, "All I have needed Thy hand hath provided."

Moses had the difficult responsibility of leading the children of Israel, and there were times when he felt his very life threatened by those angry, grumbling, complaining, disobedient people.

On one such occasion, when the people had been complaining about not having enough to drink out in that desert, God showed him what to do.

He took the elders of the children of Israel with him to the rock. (You can read the story in Exodus 17.) And at God's command, he struck the rock, and it gushed forth sweet, fresh water.

How interesting. Don't you wonder what was going on in the heads of these elders? God had told Moses what He was going to do, but these Israelite leaders didn't have a clue. They grumbled and just followed along.

I read a wonderful quote that said, "Leadership is taking people where they don't necessarily want to go, but where they ought to be." That was the responsibility Moses had. He brought them to a dry, flinty rock, and God met their need in that most unlikely of places.

The Lord's instructions to Moses were to strike the rock. The word *strike* also could be translated "to beat, wound, punish, or slaughter." The rock was struck, and out gushed enough water to satisfy thirsty millions! What a graphic picture of the Savior! The rock was broken in order to meet their need.

That is exactly what Jesus did on the cross. He was broken, and out of His brokenness we are saved—and not only saved, but satisfied. We read in 1 Corinthians 10, "They drank of that spiritual Rock that followed them, and that Rock was Christ" (verse 4).

The book of Ephesians tells us that "God raised us up with Christ and seated us with him in the heavenly realms in Christ Jesus, in order that in the coming ages he might show the incomparable riches of his grace, expressed in his kindness to us in Christ Jesus" (2:6-7, NIV).

We really have no idea of the greatness of His riches and kindness to us.

We can't begin to wrap our minds around something that vast.

It's all the more surprising when He hides His secret

storehouse of provision in seasons of our lives that seem as dry and desolate as that rock in the desert.

The water, when it gushes forth, causes us even greater wonder . . . and tastes doubly sweet.

61: WHEN TRIALS COME

Be sober, be vigilant; because your adversary the
devil walks about like a roaring lion, seeking whom
he may devour.

(1 PETER 5:8)

The attack came at Rephidim, the place where Moses had
struck the rock and a miraculous flow of water had gushed
out to meet the need of the children of Israel in the wilderness. It was a place of victory and joy, and the people had received
a fresh revelation of God's power and provision.

And that was the very moment the enemy chose to attack.

It was at that moment that "the warriors of Amalek came to
fight against the people of Israel at Rephidim" (Exodus 17:8, TLB).

So it is in our lives. It is often after a time of great blessing,
joy, and peace in our lives when the attack comes. Maybe we've
had a wonderful experience with the Lord or made some significant step forward in our spiritual lives. And while we're just
savoring that time, we're blindsided by an attack.

That was certainly how it happened for Jesus. He had just
been baptized by His cousin John when the sky was torn open
and the Spirit of God descended on Him in the form of a dove.
A voice came from heaven, saying, "This is My beloved Son, in
whom I am well pleased" (Matthew 3:17).

And what happened immediately after that? The Bible says,

"Then Jesus was led up by the Spirit into the wilderness to be tempted by the devil" (Matthew 4:1).

Again, right after that glorious moment on the Mount of Transfiguration, when Jesus spoke with Moses and Elijah and the voice of the Father once again affirmed His love for the Son, Jesus had an encounter with a determined demon at the bottom of the hill. This is something we need to remember: It is often after times of great blessing that we face our greatest challenges from the enemy.

Greg and I have experienced this over the years. We have come to anticipate fierce attacks from the enemy right after one of his Harvest Crusades. Immediately after seeing God bless so abundantly, pour out His Spirit, and bring hundreds of people to Christ, we will go through a time of intense spiritual testing. Before we began to recognize the problem, we wondered what was happening to us and didn't even know how to articulate to each other what we were going through. Both of us would go into a slump or a depression right after the final night of a crusade. It's a strange oppression that comes on our emotions and our minds, and we feel terrible.

Now that we know what to expect, we are better prepared. When an attack comes, we know how to battle it. We take up the spiritual armor of Ephesians 6, putting on the helmet of salvation and the breastplate of righteousness, holding tightly to the shield of faith. We refuse to yield to those dark feelings or to let them bring us down.

The day of spiritual victory and joy is no time to relax your guard.

It's time to double up on it.

62: AN UNGUARDED STRENGTH

Therefore let him who thinks he stands take heed
lest he fall.

(1 Corinthians 10:12)

I remember hearing a pastor say once that he would never fall to the sin of adultery because he "had such a strong marriage." Because of this wonderful relationship with his wife, he declared that this would never be an issue for him.

But it was.

Because he had been so supremely confident in this area of his life, he let down his guard and got too close to a woman who wasn't his wife. At first they were "just friends," but then one thing led to another, and the enemy attacked him in the area of his greatest perceived strength.

This same pastor later admitted that "an unguarded strength is a double weakness." He had left himself unguarded in the area of his so-called strength . . . and he was more vulnerable than he knew.

The Amalekites attacked at the point of Israel's weakest defense: It came from the rear. The enemy swooped down on the slower, weaker, and struggling ones at the back of the line. It was Israel's point of weakest defense, and they ought to have been aware of that. It's true for us, too. We must always guard the most vulnerable places in our lives. We must recognize those areas of weakness in our lives and be extremely cautious and careful to protect ourselves.

Where do you struggle the most in your life? What is your greatest area of weakness? Our spiritual enemies are aware of those vulnerabilities, too, and we need to be mindful of that.

We also need to pay attention to those areas of our perceived strengths.

As long as we are in this world, we will have an enemy, and we must be prepared to fight. We aren't walking the streets of heaven yet, and it isn't over until it's over. The world, the flesh, and the devil will be our adversaries until we step through the gate of eternity and draw in that first lungful of heavenly air.

Not long ago, that thought overwhelmed me. I thought to myself, *This is like trying to climb a greased pole. This is like running a marathon that never ends.* In that moment, the Lord spoke to my heart and said, "Cathe, when you get up in the morning, you make your bed, right?"

"Yes," I replied. "Every morning."

"And you probably will make your bed for the rest of your life. Does that overwhelm you?"

"No, Lord, that doesn't overwhelm me."

"When you get up in the morning, you brush your teeth. You bathe yourself. Every day you do this. Does that overwhelm you to think that you will be brushing your teeth and taking a shower for the rest of your life?"

I said, "No, Lord. I just take it one day at a time."

"And every day, Cathe, you feed yourself. You exercise. You try to maintain your health. You do that every day. You do your laundry, cook your meals, do your dishes. You do those things without really thinking much about them, don't you?"

"Yes," I said. "That's true. I don't usually sit down and burst into tears at the thought of having to put dishes in the dishwasher for the rest of my life. I just do it."

"Your spiritual life is like that, Cathe," He said. "Get up each morning and spend some time in My Word. Spend some time talking with Me in prayer. Spend time with Me confessing your sins, praising Me, and seeking My will for your life and how you might serve Me. Do this every day, and I will take care of the world, the flesh, and the devil. Don't you worry about that. Victory is ours."

63: OVERCOMING THROUGH PRAYER

So Joshua fought the Amalekites as Moses had
ordered, and Moses, Aaron and Hur went to the top
of the hill. As long as Moses held up his hands, the
Israelites were winning, but whenever he lowered his
hands, the Amalekites were winning. When Moses'
hands grew tired, they took a stone and put it under
him and he sat on it. Aaron and Hur held his hands
up—one on one side, one on the other—so that his
hands remained steady till sunset. So Joshua
overcame the Amalekite army with the sword.

(Exodus 17:10-13, niv)

Not only did God send Israel's soldiers into battle, but He
sent Israel's leaders into battle . . . in prayer.

The New Testament tells us to "pray in the Spirit at all
times and on every occasion. Stay alert and be persistent in your
prayers for all believers everywhere" (Ephesians 6:18, nlt).

That is what Moses and Aaron and Hur were doing on that
mountain. They were interceding on behalf of the people,
helping Moses stay at the task after he had become weary.
Prayer—and intercessory prayer in particular—is spiritual
warfare. And it is wearying work.

Do you have prayer partners? When you find yourself in the
middle of an intense battle, do you have someone you can text or

call on the phone and say, "Would you pray with me? Would you come with me to the throne of grace and agree with me there?" Or do you just get on the phone and rehearse the details of the battle in all of its gory details, going back over the difficulties you are facing?

I love that picture of Aaron and Hur lifting Moses' arms on that mountain as he grew weary in prayer. Just recently one of my friends went for a run with me. As we were jogging along, I shared a need with her. She immediately said, "Let's pray," and began taking that need to the Lord.

To be honest, I hadn't really been in a praying frame of mind. I was just telling her my sad story and didn't expect her to immediately intercede for me. But that's what she did. She was like Aaron or Hur to me in that moment, lifting my arms in prayer when I didn't have the strength to do it by myself.

Robert Murray M'Cheyne, the famous Scottish preacher, once said, "If I could hear Christ praying for me in the next room, I would not fear a million enemies. Yet the distance makes no difference; He is praying for me!"

Let that thought sink in for just a moment: *God Himself is praying for you.* Jesus the Son stands before the throne of His Father and intercedes for you. As I learned it years ago in the King James Bible, "He ever liveth to make intercession" for us (Hebrews 7:25). We need not fear a million enemies.

After the victory over Amalek, we read this account in Exodus 17:

> Then the Lord said to Moses, "Write this on a scroll as something to be remembered and make sure that Joshua hears it, because I will completely blot out the memory of Amalek from under heaven."
>
> Moses built an altar and called it The Lord is my Banner. He said, "For hands were lifted up to the throne of the Lord. The Lord will be at war against the Amalekites from generation to generation." (verses 14-16, NIV)

A banner, of course, is a flag. I love the pictures of the old monarchies in Europe and the castles they occupied. When the monarch was in residence, the servants would raise the flag over that castle so all the people in town could look at the fortress and know the king was in residence. His presence was there.

As we raise the flag of God's presence over our lives, we know the Holy Spirit is in residence there. His presence is with us, and we experience His peace and joy and wisdom beyond our own. The Lord is our banner.

Yes, each one of us has been given a measure of burdens, cares, and responsibilities, but these have been carefully measured out by the Lord Himself.

When our boys were little, as soon as they were able, they were given the responsibility of helping to unload the groceries from the car after a shopping trip. Whether it was Greg or me, when we got those groceries out of the car, we would find little things they could carry in on their own — a bag of carrots, a can of beans, or maybe a box of cereal. But we never gave them a ten-pound bag of sugar or something slippery or breakable — not until they were older and able to handle such loads.

In the same way, God knows your limitations. He wants you to participate in the work, but He knows how much you can carry. He will measure out those burdens according to what you are able to bear.

And if He gives you a load that seems too heavy to carry, He will scoop you up in His arms and carry both you *and* the load. Count on it. He knows His kids, and His eye never misses anything.

64: PREPARATION FOR SUFFERING

Consider it pure joy, my brothers, whenever you
face trials of many kinds, because you know that
the testing of your faith develops perseverance.

(JAMES 1:2-3, NIV)

James doesn't say, "*If* we face trials of many kinds"; he says,
"*Whenever* we face trials of many kinds."

Not *if*, but *when*.

James is telling his flock to be prepared for this.

The problem today is that we live in a time and culture that
does not prepare us for the reality of suffering. In bygone days
(and in other places in the world today) people were far more
realistic about suffering and trials in life.

Cultures and times previous to this one prepared their children because suffering and death were a common occurrence in
life. It wasn't a surprise as it is to us today.

Today's Western culture tells you that if you lose a spouse or
a love affair or a job, then life has lost all its meaning. In essence,
you have lost everything because life is meant to be one uninter-
rupted string of joy and pleasures.

Even though many of us as Christians have grown up with
the stories of Daniel in the lions' den, Joseph in the dungeon, and
Paul in a shipwreck, our expectations have been shaped by our
contemporary culture. Even those of us who know better often

develop a skewed attitude about what our lives should look like or feel like.

If you were to interview a fish down under the sea and ask it about water, it might reply, "What's water?" It probably wouldn't be aware of water because it is enveloped in water — soaked in its own culture, if you will.

And don't kid yourself: We are soaked in our culture, too. If we find ourselves suffering, we think we ought to sue someone. We say to ourselves, "This isn't my fault, and I shouldn't have to go through this. Someone is to blame. Someone needs to make this stop. Someone needs to make the suffering go away. I don't deserve this. I deserve to be happy and pain-free."

We are a crybaby culture, and we need to recognize that fact and toughen up a little bit. We need to see life as it really is and not as we would wish it to be or as our culture tells us it *ought* to be.

James just assumes that trials will be part of our lives as believers . . . and so should we.

65: HOW TO FACE YOUR TRIALS

Perseverance must finish its work so that you may
be mature and complete, not lacking anything.

(JAMES 1:4, NIV)

If we want to become strong, mature believers, living the life
that God intends for us, we need to respond in the right way to
the hardships, bruises, and stressful circumstances that crash
into our lives. James has nothing to say to the Christian who
thinks life always will be a bed of roses.

He begins his book by saying, "Consider it pure joy . . . whenever you face trials of many kinds" (James 1:2, NIV).

Does this sound like spiritual masochism to you? It does at
first reading, doesn't it? If a non-Christian were to read these
words, he or she might conclude that Christians aren't supposed
to ever experience emotions of sorrow, grief, pain, or sadness.
Instead, we're supposed to smile all the time and walk around in
a superficial cloud of giddiness and joy.

But that is not what James is saying.

James knew what it was to suffer as a believer. Although
many believers fled Jerusalem during the days of intense Roman
persecution, James stayed in town and endured it. He understood well tears, sorrow, and sighing. Ultimately, he would lay
down his life for his belief in Jesus.

So when James says, "Consider it pure joy," he's not talking
down to suffering people from some ivory tower. He is speaking
from the crucible of fire himself.

James is saying, "I want you to consider a new perspective about these sufferings we have to endure. I want you to look at the results of what these trials can mean in your life." In verses 3 and 4, he tells us that "the testing of your faith develops perseverance" and "perseverance must finish its work so that you may be mature and complete, not lacking anything" (NIV).

Christians don't persevere for perseverance's sake alone; there is an end in view, a goal to reach, a purpose to be fulfilled. We persevere so that our lives will be transformed. There are certain benefits and strengths and graces God wants to add to your life that He can't get into you any other way.

Think of an athlete training for an event or a student learning French who spends hours conjugating verbs. Why do they do these things? Is it just to punish the body or exhaust the mind? No, there's a point to it. The athlete trains so that she might one day ride her bike through the mountains of France and experience all the glories of such a trip. The student works at his verbs so that he might speak the French language fluently, understand their literature, and be able to have beautiful conversations.

In the same way, there is a point to all of the proving, training, and testing that God allows us to experience and endure.

What are your objectives in life? If your goal is to simply live a carefree life and get through your threescore-and-ten as painlessly as possible, then problems, heartaches, and setbacks will be nothing more than that—just bad stuff that you have to endure and get through as best you can. But if you begin to look at the trials in your life from God's perspective, then, in the very midst of your tears and pain and grief, you can taste His joy. Why? Because you know those trials are getting you closer to the goals that God has for your life.

As James writes, you will become "mature and complete, not lacking anything." In other words, God will equip you for whatever lies ahead . . . in this life and the next.

66: THE VICTOR'S CROWN

He who testifies to these things says, "Surely I am
coming quickly." Amen. Even so, come, Lord Jesus!
(REVELATION 22:20)

have a vine in my backyard called a stephanotis. It gets its
botanical name from the Greek word that means "crown."

It is gorgeous.

Those of you who have been to florist shops would recognize
it. The flowers are white, trumpet-shaped, and wonderfully
fragrant. Florists will pick the flowers off the stems on the vine
and bundle them together. In a bridal bouquet, it is fragrant and
gorgeous without any greenery at all.

Do you want to know what task God has for you in your
remaining years? Do you want to know your calling? Your
vocation?

The word *vocation* comes from the Latin word *voca*, which
means "call." At one time, people recognized that our life's work
should be something more than some job we perform from nine
to five, Monday through Friday. It is a *calling*. It is a discovery of
the purpose of your life. If you want to know what that calling
is, suffering is a way to get you closer to that goal. In fact, suffering can prepare you better than any classroom, textbook, self-
help manual, or college course you could ever take. Suffering
equips you. It turbocharges you to grow in Christ.

Again, this doesn't mean you want to suffer for the sake of suffering. When Jesus stood at the tomb of His close friend, Lazarus, He wept and was angry. Death, suffering, sin, and separation were never part of God's original plan. You and I can be angry at the suffering and pain in a fallen world and yet not be angry at God.

Romans 8:28 lays it out for us so clearly: "And we know that all things work together for good to those who love God, to those who are the called according to His purpose."

God says to us, "If you trust Me and hold on to Me through suffering, I can work things out so that your trials will be like a furnace, turning your faith into pure gold."

In the short term, God will use hardships and troubles in your life to prepare you for the challenges that lie before you in the coming days and years. But there is a long-term perspective too. In James 1:12 we read, "Blessed is the man who perseveres under trial, because when he has stood the test, he will receive the crown of life that God has promised to those who love him" (NIV).

That word *crown* in the text is the Greek word *stephanos*, which was a wreath or garland presented to a victor returning from battle. It would also be presented to an athlete who had won an event in the Olympic games. The wreath would be placed on the head of the victorious one like a crown.

One day in heaven we'll be given a *stephanos* . . . a crown of life. I don't imagine that it will be a literal crown, but no one on this side of eternity really knows *what* it will be. I sometimes imagine this crown representing what God intended our lives to be, as He planned them before the Fall, before time itself. Whatever the crown of life might be, we will one day achieve the incomparable, indescribable beauty of a face-to-face relationship with our God.

That is the long-term goal. It is the final reward.

If your value system is all wrapped up in this life, this passage will make no sense to you at all. But if you can cry out with Christians of all ages, "Even so, come, Lord Jesus!" in the midst of your trial, then you know what I'm talking about. Trials prepare you not only for this life, but also for life in the future—life in heaven.

As I've already stated in this book, I love the way Paul said it in his letter to the believers in Corinth: "For our light and momentary troubles are achieving for us an eternal glory that far outweighs them all. So we fix our eyes not on what is seen, but on what is unseen. For what is seen is temporary, but what is unseen is eternal" (2 Corinthians 4:17-18, NIV).

By the way, those "light and momentary troubles" Paul mentions included being whipped on five separate occasions with thirty-nine lashes. People often don't survive even one such scourging. Three times he was beaten with rods. He had been shipwrecked. He was hounded, harassed, and persecuted all over the Roman world. He even had been stoned and left for dead. Yet he calls all of these terrible, horrific things that had been done to him "light and momentary troubles." This great lion of an apostle suffered so much. And yet because of his perspective, he could look through his painful trials and see the eternal reward—the eternal glory, which he insisted would far outweigh whatever he had to face on earth.

Holding on to God through suffering will change your perspective, and it will make *all* the difference in facing your trials. And I don't mean just big sufferings; this applies to the smallest sufferings as well.

The girlfriend who took your best friend to lunch and didn't invite you.

The guy you have fallen in love with who won't give you a passing glance.

The times when you feel lonely and rejected, and you find

yourself thinking, *Everybody is married, but I'm not. Everybody has someone, but I have no one.*

Some may call these small sufferings, but when we are going through them, they *are* sufferings, and the Lord who loves us *does* care about these things. A sharp rock in your shoe may be small, but it hurts and may even cause you to limp. The apostle Peter said it so well: "Give *all* your worries and cares to God, for he cares about you" (1 Peter 5:7, NLT, emphasis added).

The Lord is working in our hearts, even in a time of pain or disappointment, and we can say, "Lord, even though I am rejected, even though I am left out, You never leave me out. Even though I don't have a husband, I have You, an eternal, heavenly husband. And someday at the great wedding feast of the Lamb, I will receive the crown of life *there* that I am longing for *here.*"

Gaining this perspective is no bandage or temporary fix; it is the real deal, and it leads to the eternal joy that Paul says far outweighs and outlasts every other joy.

Trials and tribulations will humble you, show you your limitations, and also give you empathy for others who are suffering. You can walk up to someone who is grieving or has lost a baby or has a prodigal child or whose husband has been unfaithful, and you can look at the pain in their faces and not be embarrassed. How do you do that unless you yourself have experienced and learned something from the suffering you have been through?

Suffering is good for us.

We don't want it, don't like it, and would rather avoid it. But in time, with God's help, we come to understand its ultimate value.

67: YOUR FIRST RESPONSE

In all your ways acknowledge Him, and He shall
direct your paths.

(PROVERBS 3:6)

When Greg and I went through the hardest days of our lives following the loss of our son Christopher, we were given so many books. We now have stacks of books on grieving. We received many letters and cards from caring people. Others sent us sermon CDs. Lots of people gave us quotes. Some of these were helpful and some not so helpful.

When you are in a season of darkness and trial, it's a little like the sport of free climbing. Have you ever watched free climbers? These men and women scale sheer rock cliffs and mountains—without ropes. When you watch them climb, it's almost as though they are glued to the side of the cliff, as they scale it so slowly you can barely see them making progress. That's how it feels in grief sometimes, or when we're in a time of stress. You are begging God for wisdom and just inching along, groping for that next crevice that will give you a handhold.

The apostle James makes it sound so simple. In James 1:5, he states, "If any of you lacks wisdom, he should ask God" (NIV). How basic can you get? If you find yourself in need of wisdom, go to God and ask Him for some!

You often hear this verse quoted when someone is up against

some personal decision: *Do I buy this house? Do I marry this guy? Do I take this job in another city?* And certainly God will guide us in such things. But the real context here is for wisdom regarding the trials that we face: *Lord, how do I manage this? How do I survive this? Lord, please show me how to get through the next day, the next hour, or the next ten minutes.* James is saying, "Ask God to give you what you need."

Even though suffering will make us mature, as James tells us, we never will outgrow this aspect of prayer. We are told to come humbly to our heavenly Father and ask for wisdom. We are to close the door to our prayer closet, get on our knees or on our faces before an all-good and all-wise God, and seek wisdom from Him, face-to-face.

Go to Him before you go to anyone else.

Before you call your best friend.

Before you visit your favorite pastor.

Before you text your sister across town.

Before you make an appointment with the counselor.

Begin by asking God and waiting on Him for the wisdom that you need. And He will give it to you.

James tells us that God will be there in those moments. You may feel that you are in a vulnerable place, but He will direct you to the next handhold or foothold. He guides you where to put your weight. He gives you the Scriptures that will get you through. He brings you to a place of safety. Your progress may seem slow to you, but He will bring you to that refuge of perspective and rest.

What gets you up the mountain may not be the same thing that gets someone else up the mountain. The handholds and footholds will be different. That is why James tells each of us to ask God for wisdom in making that climb. He knows the best route for you, although it may not be the same route that someone else has taken.

Go to God in the very smallest of trials, form that habit, and you will be more likely to seek Him during the great storms. Don't immediately run to someone else with your pain or look for help at the pharmacy. Don't go online and ask Google what to do.

Run to the Lord.

Run to Him for everything.

Make that your *first* response.

68: HIGHER GROUND

Every good gift and every perfect gift is from
above, and comes down from the Father of lights,
with whom there is no variation or shadow of
turning.

(JAMES 1:17)

Phuket, Thailand, resident Bill O'Leary got the call two minutes before the first wave hit. The underwater earthquake
had measured 9.3 on the Richter scale. One of his employ-
ees, who was on the beach where his office was located, got the
word out to him clearly. The shoreline had receded 250 meters,
boats were dry, and fish were stranded. This could only mean
one thing: A tsunami was imminent.

A two-minute warning doesn't seem like much time. Could
it really be that helpful? It was for those who listened. *Get to
higher ground, NOW!*

This is the greatest encouragement I can leave you with
today. When you are facing a spiritual tsunami, feeling abandoned and crushed under your trials, do not forget to take yourself to higher ground as fast as you can. You will find that higher,
unshakable ground in the goodness of God.

In James 1:16-17, the apostle writes, "Do not be deceived,
my beloved brethren. Every good gift and every perfect gift is
from above, and comes down from the Father of lights, with

whom there is no variation or shadow of turning."

I love that statement. There is no variation with our Father, no turning or changing with Him. God isn't good because you feel it. God is good because it is true.

Hebrews 12 tells us to fix our eyes on Jesus, "who for the joy set before him endured the cross, scorning its shame" (verse 2, NIV). Remember His goodness, revealed for all eyes for all time, on the cross of Calvary.

We are told that our God is the Father of the heavenly lights. What are the most stable things in the universe?

The stars.

Earth is spinning on its axis, and the seasons come and go. But we can always look to the stars and navigate by them. Even in the darkest woods we can navigate by the North Star.

But even the stars are changing. Astronomers tell us that the universe is slowing down by a fraction of a second with each passing year. But God, the Father of lights, never changes. He is more reliable than the North Star and more permanent than the constellations. No matter what happens in our lives or in our world, we can always navigate by Him. His goodness never changes.

When you are facing those heartbreaking trials or disappointments in your life, remember that God's goodness is more stable than the ancient stars and will go on and on after the galaxies have turned to dust. His pledge to you is that He is, and always will be, invariably good. Immovably good. Irremediably good. That means He couldn't change even if He wanted to (which He doesn't). He doesn't have bad days. He doesn't get up and say, "I have low blood sugar today. I'm going to take it out on those human beings down there." In this broken, torn, ravaged, and fallen world, we have a God who is still good. He is there for us, and He promises to always be there for us.

Yes, I know, sometimes it doesn't *seem* that He is good. We ask ourselves why He doesn't stop the pain or the stress when He has the power to stop it. Are you thinking thoughts like those? Why not just tell Him what you're thinking? Tell Him if you are feeling angry, afraid, or abandoned. After all, He knows your heart anyway. Pour out your heart to Him. You won't be saying anything more than some of the psalmists said.

Before you decide that God isn't good, however, consider two things.

First, God isn't a genie who will come up out of a lamp and grant you three wishes. Would you really want a god who did everything you told him to do? Wouldn't you rather have a God who is so vast, so wise, and so good that He will sometimes do things you and I can't always comprehend?

Second, whatever you may have lost, remember that God gave up His own Son out of love for you and love for this world. Before you decide that God has forgotten about you or doesn't care about you, I would ask you to measure whatever trial you are facing today and lay it alongside what Jesus endured on that little hill outside of Jerusalem, where He suffered and bled and died for you.

Sooner or later, it will happen. Life will kick you soundly in the teeth, and no doctor, lawyer, or counselor will fix it. This is a broken, dying world. In fact, it's terminal. But God is still good. Fix your eyes on Him. Don't be deceived. Don't wallow in self-pity. Don't accuse God angrily or rashly. When the sky darkens, the rains fall, the floods rise, and the wind rages, get yourself to the high ground.

Remember the goodness of God.

69: PRAY YOUR EMOTIONS

Trust in him at all times, O people; pour out your
hearts to him, for God is our refuge.

(PSALM 62:8, NIV)

God is less shockable than we are.

When we read some of the Psalms, we're almost taken
aback by David's candor. We might find ourselves saying,
"Really, David? You're asking God to judge your enemies and
dash them to pieces? You need to get hold of yourself!"

But God was just fine with David's honesty and his display
of emotions. In fact, David became known as "the man after
God's own heart." What He wanted from David is the same
thing He wants from us: an honest heart, poured out in its
entirety before the Lord.

I believe that God placed the Psalms in Scripture for a
number of reasons. Obviously, they contain good theology and
teach us doctrine. But one of the strongest impressions I have
gained this year as I have studied the Psalms is the conviction
that God gives us permission—and even encouragement—to
come to Him honestly.

What do we do with our tears and our fears when we find
ourselves under circumstances such as David had to deal with in
this psalm?

We bring these emotions to God in prayer and pour them
out.

I teach a women's Bible study at our church, and as I was introducing this psalm, I said, "We're all women in here, and chances are we're more emotional than the average man out there. We're more expressive, more tenderhearted, and we feel things more deeply. What we *do* with those emotions is the question. We need to learn where to take our tears and our fears."

In earlier generations in the U.S., the average person would have been told to control himself or herself . . . to deny emotions, pushing them aside, stuffing them under a calm facade . . . to "buck up" and move on with life. (In England, they called it keeping a stiff upper lip. During the bombing of London during World War II, there was a sign the British government posted throughout the city that simply read, "Keep calm and carry on.") I think that "buck up" attitude was especially true of those who lived through the Depression and World War II — my parents' generation. That generation was not prone to expressing their emotions.

My dad, while affectionate, was never very emotional. It was my mother who was always letting her emotions show. She is Spanish, so perhaps she gets a free pass in this regard. But my dad, with his English-Irish stoic attitude, didn't do that very often. He would deny his emotions and keep them under a lid. In consequence, he ended up with an ulcer.

So what is the alternative to stuffing your emotions? Could it be that the pendulum has swung too far in the other direction these days? As Martin Luther put it, "The world is like a drunken peasant. If you help him up on one side of the horse, he falls off on the other side." One can't help him, no matter how one tries. My generation — the one that came of age in the sixties and seventies — talked a lot about "being real." And if anybody questioned us on that, we would say, "I'm just going to let it all hang out. This is who I am, so you can take it or leave it."

As Christian women, we don't want to embrace either of

these extremes. We don't want to deny and stuff our emotions, nor do we want to give vent to them and let them fly all over the place.

What, then, do we do with our emotions?

We pray them.

We pray them out in the presence of God, for the ears of God. David said, "Trust in him at all times, O people; pour out your hearts to him, for God is our refuge" (Psalm 62:8, NIV).

That's the phrase: *Pour out your hearts to Him.*

When I speak of praying your emotions, I don't mean wrapping them up in tidy little theological packages. I don't mean editing them and putting them into some kind of acceptable format. When you are writing in your journal, do you ever think about people who might actually read your journal someday? Do you find yourself wanting to maybe clean it up a bit, making it sound more reasonable or spiritual?

There is no need to do that in prayer. God sees the whole of you, the entire package of your life. He sees where you have come from, He knows what you are experiencing, He reads and understands your heartbreak, your tears, and the fears you may have never expressed to another living person. He also knows what He has in mind for you and where He is taking you.

You can take the real you into His presence and say everything that is in your heart.

70: WHAT TO FEAR ... AND *NOT* FEAR

"I will teach you the way that is good and right.
But be sure to fear the LORD and serve him
faithfully with all your heart; consider what great
things he has done for you."

(1 SAMUEL 12:23-24, NIV)

Far too often we fear the wrong things in life instead of fearing God, being in awe of Him, and being careful not to displease Him.

When I think about fearing the wrong things, I am reminded of an incident from the life of a friend of mine. One night before Christmas she was shopping late—right up until the stores at the mall closed their doors. Emerging from the bright mall into the darkness of the parking lot, she realized to her discomfort that most of the cars were gone. Hurrying to her car, she slid inside and locked the door, sighing with relief. Just as she was getting ready to turn the ignition and drive away, she noticed a man walking toward her car. He was just a normal-looking guy who didn't look dangerous or threatening.

He walked up to her car window and spoke to her through the glass. Her first (and right) instinct was to protect herself and get out of there. Something told her, "This isn't quite right. Don't stay here. Go . . . *now.*"

Instead, she sat in her car as he walked up to the window.

Through her closed window, she heard the man say, "I am so sorry, but my car won't start. Battery died, I guess. Do you have any jumper cables?"

As it turned out, she did have jumper cables in the back of her car. Her God-given instinct, however, was telling her, "Do not roll down your window. Do not open the car door." But what she said was, "I really need to be going. My mother is expecting me." (Why she engaged him in conversation is beyond me, but she did.)

And then he said, "Please help me."

What happened in that moment was this: Another fear took over her more sensible fear. And that was the fear of *what he thought of her.* This guy presented himself to be in some sort of distress, and she felt bad that she wasn't even willing to roll down her window and speak to him.

So she did. She cracked her window. And as it rolled down, there was just enough room for him to reach his arm inside, unlock the door, and yank on the door handle. In what seemed like one second, he had pushed his way into the driver's seat, wrapped an arm around her neck, and put a knife blade to her throat.

At that moment, thank God, someone from the mall came walking out into the parking lot and heard her screaming. The assailant saw the other man approaching, leaped out of my friend's car, and took off running. He was later apprehended, prosecuted, and convicted.

But here is what interests me about this incident. My friend experienced two kinds of fear on that night: a good, logical fear, and then another fear—the fear of what a stranger might think of her. And that second, foolish fear overcame the wholesome and wise fear, endangering her very life.

In the same way, there are things in our lives we should fear and other things we should not fear. First and foremost, we should fear the Lord. The Bible tells us that this is "the beginning of wisdom." And the remarkable thing is that when we get that proper fear in place — which is reverence for God, a desire to not displease God, a desire to do what He commands — then we don't fear anything else.

David said, "The Lord is the strength of my life; of whom shall I be afraid?" (Psalm 27:1).

That's a statement — and a question — worth repeating every day of our lives.

71: COMFORTING OTHERS

> He comforts us in all our troubles so that we can
> comfort others. When they are troubled, we will
> be able to give them the same comfort God has
> given us.
>
> (2 CORINTHIANS 1:4, NLT)

Running from trials and difficult times never helps. Shrinking back from following our Lord and Captain into what might look like dark clouds, hard times, or demanding tasks never will produce anything. If, on the other hand, you invest your trials and tears, God will use them to change you and to change others.

Hanging in a museum in northern France is a famous tapestry called the Bayeux Tapestry. Accompanying one of the scenes on the tapestry is the inscription, "Bishop Odo, holding a staff, comforts his troops." Don't expect to find him putting his arms around his men and speaking softly and gently to them. Actually, this bishop is in full battle armor, riding at full gallop alongside his troops, waving what looks more like a club than a staff! He is encouraging, driving, and rallying his knights.

Sometimes we need to be reminded that the meaning of the word *comfort* also can be translated "strengthen" or "summon." (This doesn't have anything to do with those familiar, down-filled blankets we love on cold nights!)

When you are in the middle of a crisis, it's difficult to think of anyone but yourself (as I know so well). But I would challenge you with this hard-won truth: One of the best and most satisfying cures for your troubles is to simply follow the Lord in the midst of your pain and heartache and focus on the needs of those around you.

In the aftermath of our son Christopher's going to heaven, so many people have come up to me and wanted to talk to me about their situation — including the death of a spouse or a child — because they know what Greg and I have gone through. Most of the time, I find they want to look into the eyes of someone who understands, someone who has been there and survived.

There certainly have been times when I *felt* like replying, "Honestly, I'd rather not talk about that right now." And yes, I may have every right to reply like that. But more often than not, I sense the Lord saying to me, *"Cathe, this is your opportunity. You can take it, or you can miss it."*

Sometimes I feel as though I can see Christopher in heaven, giving me a thumbs-up and saying, "Use it, Mom. Use the opportunity."

Am I always brave about it?

No.

Do I always do the right thing and make the best choice?

No.

But when I do, I feel the smile of God.

72: STOP YOUR SPIRITUAL SLOUCHING

Satisfy us in the morning with your unfailing love,
that we may sing for joy and be glad all our days.

(PSALM 90:14, NIV)

O ut in the middle of a terrible wilderness, the Israelites were completely dependent on God for everything. And yet in Psalm 90, Moses prays, "Satisfy us . . ." And that word *satisfy* means "saturate." In other words, "Fill us up. Bring us to overflowing with Your unfailing love."

There is so much rejoicing in this verse. Moses isn't slouching his way toward eternity; he is victorious. And he is praying for even more rejoicing and gladness in his life. Look at verses 14 and 15:

Satisfy us in the morning with your unfailing love,
that we may sing for joy and be glad all our days.
Make us glad for as many days as you have afflicted us,
for as many years as we have seen trouble. (NIV)

This is the way we ought to pray when we are in a trial or when we find ourselves in a wilderness. Moses prays with such confidence. And he isn't asking for just a little happiness or a surface frosting of joy; he is asking God for real, deep-down, over-the-top joy. Don't you love his boldness here? He is saying,

"Lord, we don't want a bandage here. We don't want some fleeting amusement that will divert us for an hour or two. We want real and lasting joy and gladness in our hearts."

In verses 16 and 17, he goes on to pray for God's favor.

> May your deeds be shown to your servants,
>   your splendor to their children.
> May the favor of the Lord our God rest upon us. (niv)

He is saying, "May it be on us and on our children." Moses isn't asking only for himself, but he is looking down the years and praying for God's blessing on his children and their children, after he is gone.

Do you pray the favor of God over your children, grandchildren, and perhaps even your great-grandchildren? We're really praying for more than His favor, aren't we? We are praying for His grace on our loved ones, His unmerited favor.

That is . . . *splendor.* That is a life worth living.

There is nothing wrong with praying for joy, gladness, satisfaction, beauty, and delight for you and your loved ones. *In fact, that is the very thing to pray in the middle of your wilderness.* Don't just wring your hands and lament the fact that you are here in this world and it is hard. Pray with boldness for God's blessing and favor.

Pray for His smile on your life.

73: AT HOME IN GOD HIMSELF

Lord, you have been our dwelling place throughout
all generations.

(PSALM 90:1, NIV)

oses, throughout his long life, was a pilgrim and a sojourner.
I think that must be why he writes so movingly about God
being His refuge, or dwelling place. Moses had made a
home in God Himself:

Lord, you have been our dwelling place
throughout all generations.
Before the mountains were born
or you brought forth the earth and the world,
from everlasting to everlasting you are God. (Psalm 90:1-2, NIV)

Through *all* generations? Yes, even back to the very first
generation. Moses was the one who recorded the creation account
in Genesis 1–3. He could say, as well as or better than anyone,
that throughout all time God had been an eternal refuge for
those who would run to Him.

In Numbers 33 we read of forty-two different locations
where the nation of Israel camped during its forty years in the
wilderness. Apparently, they moved at least once a year.

I don't envy them that! I've had enough moving to last me a lifetime.

We are told that, on average, Americans move once every two years. That seems so strange to me. It didn't used to be that way. People would live in their villages and die in their villages, sometimes keeping an ancestral home for multiple generations. But it's not like that anymore.

Christians are called pilgrims too. We actually call it the Christian *walk*. It isn't the Christian settle-down-and-stay. This world isn't our home, and we're passing through on our way to our permanent home with God.

Home.

Scripture uses many metaphors and word pictures for God, but this one is especially precious to me. Through most of my childhood, until I was in high school, our family moved every two to three years — not only to different houses, but to different *countries*. We were constantly dealing with unfamiliar cultures, strange languages, and different religions. I always felt like a resident alien, out of sync and out of step with the world around me. I always had to be the new kid in school and struggled to make friends and get established.

I vividly remember moving from Thailand to Princeton, New Jersey. On the way we stopped off in the Philippines to visit my mother's family and stayed for a while with my uncle, aunt, and cousins. I really loved being surrounded with family and didn't want to leave. But the day came when all five of us kids had to get ready to board yet another plane. I can close my eyes and see my mother lining us up for the trip, all of us dressed in identical traveling clothes. I especially remember the ride to the airport, tears blinding my eyes, because I was so upset to be saying goodbye again. It seemed like my whole life had been a series of goodbyes as we moved from country to country. The idea of having a permanent home or putting down roots was a foreign concept to me, but I longed for it all the same. I was homesick for something I'd never known.

To this day, I love my home and don't leave it willingly. I feel like I am a bit of a hobbit, one of the imaginary little people in J. R. R. Tolkien's fantasies. I love hobbits, because they are such home-loving creatures. They love their cozy hobbit holes (with the kettle singing on the fire) and their familiar little villages. They like to stay home and don't appreciate travels or "adventures." They also love to eat and drink!

Yes, I've traveled with Greg on numerous occasions through the years, but I would much rather stay home. If I had my way, I would even spend our vacations at home here in beautiful Southern California. And rather than going out at night, I'd stay home to watch an old movie. Home is precious.

As Christians, however, we are not called to be permanent dwellers. In fact, our *real* home isn't here at all. We are called to a pilgrimage. The apostle Peter put it like this: "Dear friends, I warn you as 'temporary residents and foreigners' to keep away from worldly desires that wage war against your very souls" (1 Peter 2:11, NLT).

Temporary residents and foreigners.

We are travelers and partners in a great adventure with God—sojourners in this wild world—and deep within our hearts, we feel like we don't belong. We're homesick for heaven, a place we've never seen and can barely imagine. As dear as people on earth are to us, and as much as we may love and treasure familiar places, our hearts and homes should be in God Himself.

AFTERWORD

Four years ago today, at 9:01 a.m., my firstborn son, Christopher, left this world and was ushered in (as Elisabeth Elliot so beautifully put it) "through gates of splendor."

I struggle to find a way to express my four-year-old grief. It's a burden that grows ever lighter . . . and ever heavier. Like Frodo's ring, it is both treasured and dreaded.

Around his grave, under the olive tree, I've replanted flowers of fragrant lavender and rosemary. Just recently, the oxidized lettering on the stone bench began to fade. We had it reapplied and darkened it again. (Greg chose the particular font Helvetica because it was a font Christopher liked.)

Last year, the little modern birdhouse and feeder that Stella and Lucy hung in the olive tree mysteriously disappeared. Brittany replaced it.

The tree grows taller, wilder, and needs pruning every fall . . . a reminder of each passing season. We are older. His precious children are taller, more beautiful, and full of personality and talent. His brother has a wife, a family, and, just this month, a third child. This one, a boy, is named in his honor.

Life continues, and every day, every day we miss him.

Looking back, thinking about where we are now and the unusual things that the Lord has done, I am grateful . . . but not fully satisfied. What I want—and am certain I will have one day—is a restoration of all things.

> "Behold, I make all things new."
> —Jesus

Cathe Laurie
July 24, 2012

NOTES

Chapter 9: What You Have to Lose
1. See Ephesians 1:8 and 1 John 3:1 in the NIV.

Chapter 14: "Forgive Me for Marrying Him!"
1. C. S. Lewis, *The Business of Heaven: Daily Readings from C. S. Lewis* (Orlando: Harcourt, 1984), 63–64.

Chapter 19: Mirror, Mirror
1. Quoted in Roy B. Zuck, *The Speaker's Quote Book* (Grand Rapids, MI: Kregel, 2009), 34.

Chapter 20: Small Prayers
1. John Newton, *John Newton's Olney Hymns* (Minneapolis: Curiosmith, 2011), 34.

Chapter 22: Snap, Edit, Post
1. Anne Lamott, *Traveling Mercies: Some Thoughts on Faith* (New York: Anchor Books, 1999), 143.

Chapter 25: What to Do with Tears and Fears
1. Margery Williams, *The Velveteen Rabbit* (Tarrytown, NY: Marshall Cavendish Corporation, 2011), 12–13.

Chapter 34: Fifty Shades of Grey?
1. John Bunyan, *Pilgrim's Progress* (New York: P. F. Collier and Son, 1909), 16.

Chapter 43: Idol Factories

1. Timothy Keller, *Counterfeit Gods: The Empty Promises of Money, Sex, and Power, and the Only Hope That Matters* (New York: Dutton, 2009), xviii.

Chapter 48: Every Girl Knows the Feeling

1. Quoted in Lee Strobel, *What Jesus Would Say* (Grand Rapids, MI: Zondervan, 1994), 23.

Chapter 49: Honest to God

1. Quoted in Roy B. Zuck, *The Speaker's Quote Book* (Grand Rapids, MI: Kregel, 2009), 34.

Chapter 53: Driven into Joy

1. C. S. Lewis, *A Grief Observed* (New York: HarperCollins, 1961), 65.

Chapter 54: God, the Great Alchemist

1. Excerpted from the hymn, "Be Still, My Soul," by Katharina von Schlegel.

Chapter 56: The Fruit of a Thousand Choices

1. Nancy Leigh DeMoss, *Choosing Gratitude: Your Journey to Joy* (Chicago: Moody, 2009), 68.

Books by Greg Laurie

Visit www.kerygmapublishing.com